# Fresh Out of
# High School
## into the
# Workforces

O Monte

authorHOUSE®

AuthorHouse™
1663 Liberty Drive
Bloomington, IN 47403
www.authorhouse.com
Phone: 1 (800) 839-8640

Published by AuthorHouse 08/20/2016

ISBN: 978-1-5246-2517-7 (sc)
ISBN: 978-1-5246-2518-4 (hc)
ISBN: 978-1-5246-2516-0 (e)

Library of Congress Control Number: 2016913564

Print information available on the last page.

# Table of Contents

# Introduction

I REMEMBER BEING ASKED TO supervise three young professionals with three different assignments was assigned to work without a supervisor. Now it was my responsibility to make sure they succeeded. Luckily for me while I was in the army and I had already gained experiences in all three appointed jobs. One was a weapon professional, Chemical professional, and the other was mail handler professional.

I was employed in the army for many years and also employed by several civilian companies. I actively participated in many leadership positions, mentored and coached many junior professionals to succeed, and represented our company's brand.

Some of my workplace experiences are illustrated throughout most of this book in stories that are not all dramatic, but they are different and relatable to those who are becoming leaders and to those who are leaders in the workplace. There are no textbook answers to managing employees and the workplace. This book tries to identify problems important to helping leaders and employees succeed through the lessons I've learned. Which are scattered through the text at the end of each story within the various chapters.

I developed a creeds list for supervisors and management to help manage their employees better. I also selected some workplace subjects such as how to create better awards, skills and abilities that make good leaders, workplace tips that help manage employees, job interview tips, and more. Supervisors and managers have to play the hand that is dealt to them from top management. This book was inspired by experience gained years earlier to help organizations' personnel relations strategies succeed.

CHAPTER 1

# "Fresh out of High School and into the Workforces"

BACK IN THE EARLY SEVENTIES, instead of making me stay home with her my, grandma Duck (who babysat Aunt Julia and me for the family) allowed me to walk to the cotton field with three recent high school graduates: my aunts Rosina, Carrie, and Marry. It was Friday, payday everywhere. I watched my aunts pick cotton in the hot sun and got paid at the end of that day. Later on, we all picked vegetables all day for small amounts of money.

Uncles Ulysses and James, my two younger uncles, also were recent high school graduates. They picked cotton as well because everyone who graduated from high school picked cotton as a first job. As time went on, Ulysses and James found other employment and managed to retire years later; so did my aunts.

I had one other aunt; her name was Susie-May. Like Grandma Duck, she was a stay-at-home mother. Aunt Susie-May lived next door to

Grandma Duck, and one of her routines was checking on Grandma to make sure she had help if she needed it.

There was also more family: Uncle Jacey and Uncle Robert each served in Vietnam. Surviving that war positioned them to become established home owners.

Long before my aunts and uncles worked in the cotton fields, my father the oldest brother, had to pick cotton. Years later he went on to managed to retire from a full-time job. I was about 16 years then. When he was working his full-time job, he also worked two part-time jobs. When he was finished for the day, he sometimes would drive his car to the cotton fields and offer us a ride home. Picking cotton was a family way to work and get paid enough money to purchase back-to-school clothing, food, and we always earned enough money to go to the Annual Fall Fair year after year.

After the invention of the combine, we had to stop working in the cotton fields as much.

I did not know it at the time, but my uncles and aunts had taught me something valuable: to work hard, have fun doing it, and get paid for working.

It was hard times and sad times for us all when Grandpa Sweet went on to be with the Lord on his birthday. Grandpa was a hardworking railroad man. He always came home from work for the weekends. It was the only time I saw him. He visited my dad, and sometimes they sat and watched a baseball game and took a short nap. Grandma Duck kept everyone together as best she could, and she went on to be with the Lord years later.

Like any farmer and business owner, Mr. Clarkson liked to improve his business and make more money without terminating his employees. He found it impossible to keep everyone, though, and they already had known the bad news was coming before the fall harvest time.

Agriculture's newest farm-equipment invention was called the combine vehicle. It would be the demise of all field handworkers, and every field worker knew it once he or she had seen the vehicle in action picking cotton at an alarming rate. No worker picking cotton could ever match its speed. Some of the field-handworkers would move up north to find jobs that did not require picking cotton. Everyone in the community knew it was time for a change in the cotton industry. The gin manufacturing machine was not operating enough, because people were not picking cotton fast enough; therefore, not enough cotton bales were being produced to take to the city market once a week.

The combine was purchased by Mr. Clarkson and right away it was buzzing up and down the cotton fields. By the end of each day, it delivered lots of cotton for ginning. My cousins and my brother and I were allowed to pull weeds from the many soybean fields for some coins; it was better than getting no money. My aunts and uncles had found career jobs by then.

Soon we were all going to graduate from high school. When I was old enough to secure my own job, I got one working after school and during the summer. These jobs paid barely twenty-six dollars every two weeks; again, it was better than no money. Each day, I walked five miles to get to Grandma Betsy's house by dark to cut stacks of wood for her morning fire.

The economy seemed to start improving when I graduated from high school in 1977. Like my aunts and uncles working in Clarkson's cotton fields, I purchased my new back-to-school clothing, and I helped my mother purchase my graduation cap and gown. As the young man I had grown into, I wanted more money. I also wanted somewhere to go; living in a small town got old very fast.

My parents divorced before I completed high school, and my grades slipped often. With the help of one of my teachers, I did manage to lock in a low C grade and graduate from high school. I went straight into the United States Army.

I was seventeen at that time. My résumé would have read like this: I knew lots about walking and standing around in the cotton field, picking vegetables, pulling weeds, picking up roadside trash, and being a part-time janitor. My technical skills would have read like this: very little experience with typing on the new IBM electric typewriter.

The Apple computer was new, and there was a strong possibility it could provide jobs, but I had not developed enough skills growing up to fit into any industries except for the labor workforce and the military. It was time for me to move on with my life like everyone before me.

I chose not to attend college because I felt I did not read well enough to maintain good grades. Although I had good art skills, the military was my choice to get employed, get paid, and travel.

My dad signed my enlistment contract papers while I was only seventeen and still in high school. My mother drove me and my older brother to Fort Jackson, South Carolina, through Gate Number One and on to the Personnel Processing and Examination Center. It was o dark 30. We said good-bye and proceeded to walk into the building. Later on that day, my brother and I both received our orders to travel to our respective combat trainings. My brother flew to Fort Knox, Kentucky, and I took a five-minute taxi ride across the post to sign in for training.

## CHAPTER 2

# Students in Training

NEAR THE END OF COMPLETING my eight weeks of combat training, I found out that I'd flunked several important tests prior to entering training. That failure set me back about three weeks from attending Advanced Individual Training (AIT), the important phase of training.

My travel status changed to redirect me to sign into the Special Training Camp (STC). STC helped develop failing students who did not apply themselves enough to raise their academic scores to gain a pass to attend AIT.

I thought STC was a Special Forces program. Others laughed at me and said "STC" was a special education program for dummies. Although I always knew I was a C-minus student, I was not a dummy. Their comment was not funny to me.

On my bus ride after graduating from BTC, I was visualizing going to a place where there was fresh-cut, manicured grass and a new building to live in. Boy, was I so wrong! Instead, what I saw was an old, wooden, World War II two-level, tin-roof sleeping quarters. After I had arrived and gotten settled in my room, I was selected to lead students. That sounded exciting and easy.

In a few days, my responsibilities changed more than I ever would have imagined. I had to take on mentoring students who were having a hard times adjusting to being away from their homes and adapting to this hurry-up-and-rush army way of life.

Every day was getting more stressful, marching (walking) twenty minutes to and from school every day. I made sure all the students cleaned and organized their rooms and kept them free of trash and that everyone got along. I often neglected my homework, ensuring that everyone else had completed their homework and routine living assignments.

Two weeks later, my motivation was down, and so was everyone else's. I asked myself how I was supposed to lead them and keep up with my homework.

My drill sergeant was my mentor. Drill Sergeant Page was his name. He always would say to me in a loud voice, "Son, take care of the student," and "Check on the students' behaviors every day, and strengthen the ones that are weak."

Together every morning, Drill Sergeant Page and I inspected the twenty-five men's living areas and outside around the buildings until I understood all my responsibilities. Then we would conduct the standing-in-ranks inspections, and I would walk (March) the soldiers to school singing likable songs (cadies) as the drill sergeants would do; that was a fun thing to do. By now, I had gotten all my routines and responsibilities right and become overconfident, cocky, and forgetful of taking care of my students. More importantly, I had forgotten that I was a student in training also. I loved my stay in this special training camp. The drill sergeants allowed me to act out like they did, so I felt the power, and it felt good. I liked it so much there. But then my group graduated without me and moved on to sign in at AIT.

I was now handling the new arrivals. I got the attention of one new arrival who did not like me. He was much older than I was, and he began to express his dislike for me. He called me a kiss-up. I felt he was right. And that hurt my feelings, but I did not let him know it.

I had a loud and revolting acting character that intimidated most new students into doing without thinking. I thought there was nothing wrong with being that way because the drill sergeants got paid to act that way.

By now I had racked up more time in the Special Training Camp than anybody else ever had. I was all caught up with power tripping. I visited Drill Sergeant Page to figure out where I stood as far as my graduation date. I was told to hit the books and speed it up and graduate. While I waited to graduate, I continued to speak out loud to soldiers, intimidating every soldier I could. I could not help it; I loved it.

One morning while the soldiers stood outside in formation waiting for me to inspect their uniforms and walk them to school. One of the newest students, eighteen year-old Private Bubba Dew, thought he needed to express just how he felt about me. He had had enough of my cockiness and know-everything attitude. As I was yelling directly into buck Private Bubba Dew's face, he leaned backward, and clenched his fist, and took a hard swing at my head, and missed me because I was alert enough to duck after I felt the wind from his arm swing. He was serious.

That morning, my cocky attitude ended. Bubba Dew was quickly pulled from the formation and yelled at by a drill sergeants. He was ordered to wait inside the main office for disciplinary actions. The charges were serious and pending just that fast. Private Bubba Dew was released and walked to class by himself. He wondered what trouble he had caused himself. All because of my desires to act like one of the drill sergeants.

I felt bad for Bubba Dew. He had just started his career, and now he stood a good chance of going back home, being jailed for some time, or being processed out of the army. Later that day I asked the drill sergeant to ask management to not file charges against Private First Class Bubba Dew. Management dropped all charges on him. See, I believed I'd abused my leadership position, and so did the drill sergeants; they allowed me to have too much power over the later groups. I changed my leadership ways because I was only acting out when I was a student in training with additional duties.

> **Lesson Learned:** Don't take advantages of employees to satisfy your own personal agendas, and don't be so seriously about yourself when put into a position of leading people.

We call Drill Sergeant McQueen" the morning wake-up drill sergeant"; once he entered the building, you knew it right away. He always went straight to his office and played Vietnam music of weapons firing and bombing sounds over the speaker systems throughout the sleeping quarters (barracks) very early in the morning to wake us up.

I believed he was this kooky Vietnam infantryman still stuck on the battlefields of Vietnam, and he had a crazy way of letting us know it. He was all-ways inside the building early in the mornings, and that was our sign that it was time to get up, and get moving, and you knew it right away. We knew to makeup the beds and take a quick shower before Drill Sergeant Mc-Queen make it to our area. If your bed was not properly made and he saw it, when you returned, you would find your mattress, sheets, pillow, and blankets all thrown onto the floor. And if you were still sleeping in, Drill Sergeant Mc-Queen would be throwing you and your bed to the floor while on you were sleeping in it. The year was 1978, and leadership got even stranger.

Captain' Clark, our Commander and executive leader, was the comedian-type leader that kept you laughing: he made you feel like wanting to be on his team. Anytime he spoke to us, he'd entertain us, and we understood it to be serious business all at the same time. He said, "If I tell you something twice, remember it." Got that? What? Say what? Captain Clark would make us wait for his punch line, which was followed by the sound of a Billy-goat (bahaa). On Fridays at five o'clock, just after mail call, we would be waiting outside standing on the sidewalk waiting for Captain Clark to speak and release us for the weekend.

His speeches were a fun time, and mail call was a fun time also. Captain Clark liked giving out our mail to us. This way he could try out his jokes on us and use his Billy-goat sounds. This was Captain's Clark's way of checking his students' morale because everyone laughs at mail time. Captain's Clark would call your name out loud, and when you answered back, that was the way he wanted it. He then threw your mail upward toward you, up high into the air, and your mail would not fall directly to you ever. He got a big kick out of watching you not catch your mail. It was just another fun break time away from the real work. We had some simple fun together, and I can still smile about it. For every piece of mail he threw into the air, there was one of his stupid Billy-goat! Sounds again, and big laughter always followed.

Captain Clark authorized those who liked smoking cigarettes to do so when he was late coming to speak, and he would allow smokers to take a puff to relax themselves before releasing us for the weekend on Fridays. It was about the only time when we could light up a cigarette and chat and smoke together. If you got caught smoking any time earlier during the week, you were punished by any drill sergeants that caught you. They would not let you extinguish your cigarette; you had to keep it lit and inhale and exhale while doing x amount of exercises of their choice until the drill sergeant got tire or until you finished your cigarette.

On Fridays when the safety briefing was finished, Captain Clark would release everybody, and we would rush our way upstairs to grab our things for that weekend, then race back downstairs, moving quickly to get out of each other's way to get to gate number one to catch the city bus or the next cab moving.

> **Lesson Learned:** Find a unique way to motivate your employees and keep the workplace from becoming mundane.

Three weeks later, I fell short of class academics standards because I was getting very sick from the germs floating around in our sleeping area, where more than male and female lived on two different floors. Poor air ventilations was the cause of my illness.

I was hospitalized for about three weeks with strep throat. I returned from the hospital to find out I had fallen too far behind to graduate with my classmates. I was told I was being transferred to the Unit Supply School. Senior Instructor Sergeant Smith was my school instructor for the next three weeks. If I did not pass this school, it was the end of the road for me; I was surely going back home to find other employment.

Sergeant Smith, had a salt-and-pepper, small Afro waring. His uniform was always freshly starched, more than any other instructors. He wore cleaned, shiny black boots, and walked with much confidence, speaking loudly with his deep voice that carried outside the classroom. He wore more stripes than any other classroom instructor, I guess because he was the senior instructor.

Just three weeks later nearing the end of the course, when Sergeant Smith said to me, "You know, you're ready to fail this course", but not on my watch, you shit-head," he lost his balance and tried to keep himself from falling over my desk. "Your ass is failing this class! You remind me of my hardheaded son," he said for everyone to hear.

"I see your records shows that you have an appreciation letter from a Drill Sergeant Page down at that Dummies Camp, "he said, referring to the Special Training Camp., "What in the hell were you doing in that place"?"

Sergeant Smith was not aware he spit. One of his other problems was that he took drinks of alcohol on the job away from us when he was teaching us. We did not know at the time that he drank at work. Not until one morning, when we all witnessed someone of higher rank pull Sergeant Smith to the side and tell him to "take your drunk ass home now!" He left the classroom. That was the last time we saw Sergeant Smith teaching any supply classes.

Sergeant Smith's awards were displayed all over on the classroom walls. They proved him to be the best instructor on more than five occasions. That was all good, but he had a drinking problem, and the students and the other instructors knew it. He knew how to teach his classroom subjects thoroughly because he had made a career out of teaching the same subjects.

I once saw Sergeant Smith two years later standing at a bus stop downtown, it seemed as if he was waiting to catch a city bus. He was wearing his military fatigue jacket and blue jeans. It seemed as if he had retired from the army. Before Sergeant Smith departed, he tutored me and a few others after class. My scores improved well enough to meet the class standards, and we graduated on time.

---

**Lessons Learned:** When correcting someone, don't do it in front of others, ask that person to step aside to a much more private space.

---

CHAPTER 3

# A Rare Event in My Life

MANY OLD SOLDIERS BELIEVED THE Ninth Infantry would return to Vietnam because of the ax murder incident that happened on the world's most dangerous boarder, called the "DMZ in 1976.

When I arrived to A Company, the Ninth Infantry Division, the time was early 1978. I signed in at age eighteen year old, fresh out of AIT and fresh out of high school. I knew nothing about what had happened on the DMZ before then. The on duty noncommissioned officer for that day told me. Do not unpack your bags, son", "you're going to South Korea to fight the North Koreans." He explained to me, "When you were still in high school, two Americans army officers were killed while supervising a work detail on the DMZ". "Be ready" to fight: that's all I can tell you for now, young blood." I was having troubles processing what I'd just heard. This news made me start wondering what I had gotten myself into. The sergeant put fear in my heart to where I started looking to find the nearest pay phone booth. I wanted to call home to my mother to say good-bye, but I decided not make that phone call. I walked away and went to my temporary room to get some sleep.

Saturday morning came, and I lay around a long time and missed the scheduled breakfast and lunch meals right underneath my room.

My room was above the dining facility, and I could smell the food, but I was more tired from graduation

Monday morning a co-worker knocked on my door and introduced himself to me. He later showed me around the organization, and we met other coworkers.

Every day that week was a new experience. Nothing more was said about going to fight the North Koreans, so I stopped thinking about it, until soldiers started showing their hate for being in the army.

Many of the soldier in A Company believed our battalion was going back to Vietnam because of all the rumors spread fast that we were going back to fight.

Many of the younger soldier were badly influenced by negative soldiers preparing to depart the army because of the fear of the possibility of the Ninth Infantry returning to war. Many slowly became withdrawn and stopped socializing at the company's large gatherings.

To keep morale high, the commander scheduled Friday' volleyball games; and other indoor/ -out-door sports games with other companies to keep us competitive and motivated.

We would load up everybody after work on military five-ton trucks and meet on North Fort. Alpha Company was known for having the heavyweight and lightweight installation boxing champs. This time we wanted the volley-ball championship, but it did not happen. The soldiers did not want to play anymore. Some days, you could hear someone say things like, "Re-enlist? "I don't think so". "For what? To get killed?" I am going back home before the shit hits the fan" (meaning war was coming)" One day, these guys' anger really got everyone's attention.

They had thrown a pair of their army boots up high, to where it was caught on the telephone wire or the electricity wire line. On the bottom of each boots you could see three white letters: "FTA". This was their newest way to express themselves about how badly they felt about the whole army.

When you saw the swinging boots, it meant someone was preparing to go home or they had already left the building for good.

Religion was important to me, I believed a good army leader believed in God, like sports, and went to church regularly.

During the early 70s, churches outside military installations worldwide were not integrated. So I set out walking on the installation looking for a church to attend. I walked because I was used to walking a lot back home, and besides that, I had no car.

I learned there was a Catholic Church ten minutes' walking distance from my barracks (home, so I decided to start attending that Catholic Church's services on Sunday mornings. I enjoyed the Catholic services three weeks in a row. I wore casual-type clothing, which was cool. I felt comfortable in; my blue jeans and sweaters, which was my choice, and nobody frowned on me about dressing that way. It was the right attire for walking in the cold weather. Back home, my church would not have understood me wearing blue jeans to church.

At the church prayer breakfast, I was enjoying my meal until the priest stood up from the table, reached into his pocket, pulled out a cigarette's and lit it. He talked and smoked as he talked to us about various subjects. I do not remember what the subjects were because I was thinking so much. I thought that moment was an awkward and disrespectful moment for a non-smoker like me.

I was surprised to see a small group also light up their cigarettes. It was 978s, and in most of the seventies, people smoked inside buildings and almost anywhere they wanted to. Nobody said anything about smoking, and neither did I. One week later it was time to break bread and drink wine together in remembering Jesus Christ, our Lord. I sat in the back of the church as always. I could see people up front drinking from the same goblet of wine, and that made me feel sick, back home in the South, we would not sip wine from the same cup, certainly not after someone else.

I had a bad feeling about drinking from the same cup. The thought of catching AIDS or something that would make me sick or I could die. This weighed heavily on my mind. Nobody really knew what AIDS was. I just knew AIDS killed people. I excused myself immediately, and I never came back to that church.

I set out walking again, but this time in a different direction to find a different church on this huge military installation. I found a nondenominational church and returned the next week to attend their services. I enjoyed their services, but the church songs they sang took me some time getting used to. Back home at our church Saint Mark Baptist, the music and songs were the best and still are today.

Some of the senior members questioned me too often, I though, about me not showing up to church on a regular basis. They made me feel like that church was my primary responsibility, which the army was. And the army demanded much of my personal time even on Saturdays and Sundays. Back then, I gave up going to this church and other churches all together until way later in life.

There were a few positive seasoned female leaders who said good things about the army and God to young soldiers like me. They said, "Take College courses whenever you can." Others said, "Go to all the military schools when they tell you to; "it will help you get promoted sooner." So I took their advices, and I did get promoted sooner, just like they said.

I found out those females were very important people in A Company.

We trained, sometimes outdoors, for sixty days a year preparing for war. For the next three years. I thought we would be deploying to go fight somewhere.

When I had weekends off, I ate at some of our leaders' homes. One interactional couple invited a few of us to their home to see how they were living together. I thought they were a happy couple. They showed us the new microwave they had just purchased and turned it on to show us how it worked. It was so impressive, but I was skeptical of eating food from it.

Technology had produced something new to make our eating habits at home much easier. But I lived in the barracks as a single man, and I could not make that adjustment. I was truly comfortable living above the dining room, where I could get a hot meal anytime.

Although we never went to war, the threat was real, I went back to visit my mother to tell her I had signed up to be stationed closer to home.

**Lesson Learned**: Before rumors spread too far, control them.

# CHAPTER 4

# Toxic Employees (Smart Dummies)

PAPERWORK WAS APPROVED AND IN motion for me to return to Fort Jackson and be promoted to sergeant.

My first hard business decision was firing Specialist Glory Pitman. She was the first and last employee that I had to fire in my entire army career. Specialist Glory Pitman was someone I thought was trustworthy. It turned out she was very dishonest, to the point where I could not keep her around my workplace. I discovered Specialist Pitman was involved in selling my training equipment to the young students in training to get extra money for herself. Once students in training informed Specialist Pitman they had lost their assigned training equipment, they became an easy target for her to get money from.

While conducting my weekly inventory, there were shortages on every item in storage. The next week brought the same results. This was how I found out something was wrong by physical counting. But

I did not know why. I found out when a student walked into my office and, handed me cash money to pay for his lost equipment. The young student said he was told by Specialist Pitman this was the procedure to replace lost training equipment. She explained; "Give me cash money, and I will give you a pillowcase from our storage room that same day." I immediately walked the young student to our first sergeant, Sergeant Allen, and told the student to repeat to our first sergeant what he had just explained to me. He did, and the first sergeant called Specialist Pitman the next morning because she was off that day.

I set the student down and made him put his full name and Social Security number on a cash collection voucher. I instructed him to take this form to the finance officer and then go to the post laundry and pick -up a new pillowcase.

I said, "Come back here with your receipt to be filed in your personal file." Without any more questions, we thanked the soldier and allowed him to return to his training.

It was agreed to not seek harsh punishment under military laws because Specialist Pitman was already suffering financial hardships. Removing her from the organization to get a fresh start in rebuilding her army career was less painful and embarrassing than her going to jail or putting her out of the army. She left the company for good to work at the motor pool pumping gas to fill up military vehicles.

In 1982 that seemed to be fair punishment. Weeks later my inventory counts remained the same; shrinkage had stopped. With Specialist Pitman gone, I inherited responsibilities. I worked my butt off balancing my responsibilities and hers. But that was just the beginning of my problems. Specialist Pitman set me up by hiding a very important memorandum document that I needed to read immediately and take action on. That document had a suspense date that I missed, and I was in trouble big time for not following up. My managers threatened to remove me from office. Instead, I forfeited a portion of my pay, and I was temporarily barred from re-enlisting back into the army. Weeks later, I found that document under the in-box located on my desk right in front of me. It was there on my desk all that time. The colonel's secretary said she set the document in our in–box. "I remember Specialist Pitman was picking up her mail."

First Sergeant Jones transferred to our company. More trouble was coming our way! We thought hopefully it was going to be great having one more person around, but he would prove us wrong quickly. None of us knew any information about First Sergeant Jones. Once all of his personnel papers were filed., the inside file clerk shared with us and it was clear that the first sergeant was evading trouble he had gotten himself into while he was assigned to the other company he was transferred from. His assignment with us was going to be short because he was due to submit his retirement package.

He introduced himself and asked many questions when he left, but he did not ask a single question pertaining to us; it was as if we did not directly work for or with him.

We all thought it was important that he know something about the people he was going to be supervising, but it was apparent that he did not care about leader-employee bonding. We could have been being oversensitive, but that was the way we felt about it during that time.

First Sergeant Jones always loudly questioned one of us like we were back in boot camp. He was always would bringing your personal situation to everyone's attention. It seemed he was not happy about anything we did. He never said anything positive to us, not even a good greeting of the day. He demanded things be done much faster than normal. Why? We could not figure that out. We just did what he wanted.

We could not understand his leadership reasoning. We all believed he acted like an overpaid jerk. Motivation in our workplace declined, and everyone stopped believing in this crazy man who was stuck in stupid gear driving up everyone's blood pressure.

Weeks later, First Sergeant Jones called an impromptu meeting. I dropped everything and locked the doors, cleared the people out of my office, and got yelled at for being one minute late to his importune meeting. It did not seem fair to me, and that day I had had it with him.

He stood there talking as loud as he could. Then he reached to his belt and pulled from his knife holder a nine inch knife. He then bent over, reaching toward the bottom of the office wall and. begin scraping the black paint off the wall with his knife.

After he got enough black paint flakes on it, he got as close as he could to each of us one by one. Breathing hard, he held that knife close to each of our faces to view the paint flakes. This was a scary moment for me, and I am sure the others thought likewise.

He said out loud, "You see this"? "You see this, you"? "Black is a disgusting color, and I don't like it"! I want it removed!" "Removed now from these walls and repainted with a nicer color," "immediately, "He made his point very clear about the color black. He drove my stress level off the charts that day.

The elder co-worker Sergeant Evens called us aside the next day one by one to a meeting to establish facts and make a complaint to get rid of First Sergeant Jones. This office was a diverse group who shared their disappointed feelings about First Sergeant Jones. At advice from our group leader, we filed a workplace harassment claim to the Inspector General and Equal Opportunity Department. That complaint proved that First Sergeant Jones said he hated the color black! And we took that very personally because of how we had to examine his knife up close in our faces.

Within just a few days of our complaint, First Sergeant Jones was gone. "Thank you Lord," he was fired from his leadership role as our first sergeant. He left really angry, and we never saw him again. Thank you, Jesus".

**Lesson Learned:** Reprimand those smart dummies who are dishonest and toxic to the workplace because they will often violate workplace ethics, Bottom-line, their ego gets in the way of their logical thinking.

CHAPTER 5

# Intelligence in the Pacific

COLONEL JOE CARTER, EXECUTIVE COMMANDER., was responsible for over one thousand employees' civilians and soldiers in three collocated departments minutes apart. He was a "be all you can and take care of the soldiers" type of leader. I believe he genuinely cared about people, because he spend time with people to prepare to get things done right. Although the colonel was rarely in his office day after day, he would be seen talking with many of his employees throughout each day.

The colonel would get office phone calls throughout the day, and Sergeant Leroy and Specialist Patty saved his messages and briefed the colonel when he was back in his office.

Leroy and Patty were the colonel's office clerks, and I was the supply clerk, whose office was below them. One day the colonel sat us all down and gave a short office ethics training class on how to answer telephone calls professionally.

"When answering the phones, guys," he said, "say the name of this company first", "then your rank and full name next," and lastly. "May I help you? Sir or madam?" This is how to answer telephones the proper way. Say it as professionally as you can." The colonel would always go into a teaching mode to immediately correct you with on –the-spot corrections while demonstrating respect to you.

The colonel was always the first one in the office. He would meet you coming in. He greeted everyone almost every day. If we all were in, he would say, "Good morning guys." If he saw us individually, he would greet us one by one with a handshake. I believe his greetings were genuine. The colonel liked having small talks with everyone he came in contact with.

The colonel was a leader with a competitive spirit. I would see him in the gym during our lunch hour. He played racquetball with other officers or basketball with those of lesser rank) and the civilian' workers. I would here other say, He is always a good sportsman."

When I had a chance, I would say to them, "The colonel is my boss." Another thing, if someone had a moment to talk with the colonel, he would quickly go into a teaching mode; and that was just him being a colonel unlike any other colonel I have ever met.

One Friday about one o'clock in the afternoon I was walking to the bus stop to ride the next bus going to Pearl City. When I got to Pearl City, I would have to purchase a transfer ticket going to Red Hill Honolulu, where my home was. Colonel Carter drove past me, stopped and backed up, and asked me why was I was waiting for the bus. He also asked, "Where is your car?"

"My car is scheduled to arrive next week, "sir," I replied." the colonel said to Me., "My wife and I live on the other side of Red Hill, I would be glad to give you a ride home." "Just jump inside."

I felt relieved to know I was going to be home early. I said, "Thank you, sir, "and he right away started talking. The conversation was about sports and family matters. The colonel and his wife, had been together for a long time and traveled together to many faraway places, and he did not mind sharing this personal life experience information with me. I respected him more for that.

On the ride home, as we were approaching the Red Hill entrance, the colonel began to talk about the newer generation and the older generation of workers. The Colonel said, "You will have to supervise this newer generation someday. I may not be around to see it with you. My generation, we are going to fade away." He went on to say, "When I was about your age, my father said to me", "Every parent raises their kids so they can make more money than the parents did".' Why am I telling you this? Because it's true". Right now you make more money than your parents do and more than most people your age. The military gives us the best life and lessons to teach to others who will listen." I was thinking he must be talking about my twenty year-old generation.

The colonel was way ahead of me on this subject, this was only1983. When we came to my bus stop, it was walking distance from my home. I said. "I can make it from here. I'll see you at work tomorrow morning, sir." That was the end of my ride and a valuable mentoring moment.

The colonel providing much helpful advices to me. It felt like he was playing a dad or big brother role. It was great to be on his staff. I had thoughts that I could never talk to anyone back at the office about my marriage problems, which were very few. My wife and I had just married, and any pointers I could get were welcome. The colonel and the Command Sergeant Major were very important executive leaders who cared about allowing employees get the job done without them having to be involved. My leaders were cool old Soules, and that's how I wanted to be when it was my turn to become a leader of people.

> **Lesson Learned:** Be a team player and share a few minutes talking with your employees to show them that you really care about them because they represent you and the company brand.

# CHAPTER 6

# A Cry for Help

I WAS ABOUT THIRTY YEARS old, supervising fourteen much younger soldiers, when one of them and I experienced one of the scariest moments of our lives. I made the decisions right away to put my life in danger to save his life and those of others nearby who could have been killed. This was not on the battlefield, but in the Republic of South Korea. There is a saying that goes like this: "The boys and girls are stationed down south, and the men and women are stationed up north."

As usual I spent my lunch hour eating at the dining hall with my team. All of us had two assignments while in Korea; our responsibility was to work down south and return back up north and the go back home.

One day after lunch I was walking outside the lunchroom with the intention of getting into my truck to drive back to our worksite like always. But on this day, I heard a cry for help over the noise two –and-half -ton truck engine. I ran quickly toward the cry for help and found a truck stuck on the railing. I jumped onto the side door panel, looked the driver in his eyes, and said, "We are going to get this truck off the railing." I was scared, and I guess he was also.

The driver was my specialist, eighteen year-old Specialist Yhonny Rodriguez, the kid from New Jersey. It looked like the truck would go over the four –foot railing any minute now straight down the nighty degree hillside into the administration offices below us. I yelled loudly, "we can do this." Yhonny put the vehicle in neutral gear, and the vehicle engine noise changed to a much calmer sound. Yhonny pushed the gearshift in reverse. I yelled out, slowly take your foot off the brake, "and he did.

The vehicle slowly rolled backward and dropped back into its parking space. I said to Yhonny, "Tell me what happened." With fear still in his voice, he said, "I cranked up the truck, and it jerked upward onto the railing. I don't know why, and I don't know how I stopped it from going over."

Near the end of the workday, Specialist Rodriguez and I sat down together and talked about the truck incident. Specialist Rodriguez realized that day it was entirely his fault; he could've killed himself and many others in the offices below. He said, "I made a big mistake today, Serge." Yes, you did, "I said, "but 'there were no damages to the vehicle, no damage to the railing, and nobody got killed or hurt. "Don't let this happen again.", "Understand"?"

He said, "It won't happen again, Sergeant."

Specialist Yhonny Rodriguez had arrived in Korea months earlier than the others, He had been there a long time already, and he never traveled back home for a break.

For that reason, I did not seek harsh punishment, but I did talk man-to-man with him. I did all the talking.

He said, "I feel bad because it was my fault. Nothing like this will ever happen to me again never again, Serge."

My team did almost everything together. We worked long hours repairing and modifying combat fighting vehicles and getting them ready for rail shipping. The destination was the training site, and combat training zones up north. This went on for a consistent eight weeks. Before returning home, awards were in order. I received two awards for managing this a team, and everyone else received one award; they had worked harder than I did. We earned awards for our times in a tough environment away from family.

**Lesson Learned:** Sometimes working employee's for long, unorthodox hours can cause them to not be so alert to what they should be doing.

CHAPTER 7

# Overjudging My Employees

EXECUTIVE OFFICER COLONEL BROWN (FORTY-THREE-YEARS old) asked
Me., Sergeant Weston (thirty-seven years old). "Did you notice Private
First Class Home's (nineteen years old) haircut today?"

"I said, "No. mad 'am." "May I ask what's wrong with it?"

"I want you to find out and call me with your findings."

I said, "Okay, mad 'am." "*Okay, I am in trouble now*, I thought to
myself, but Private First Class Homes never got himself in trouble.

The colonel was everyone's manager (mom or boss). Like every great
manager, did lots of checking and following ups procedures.

When I returned to my office, I observed Private First Class Homes
sitting at his desk. I spoke with him and cleverly observed his haircut. I saw
nothing wrong with him having a bald head because I was baldheaded.

It was 1995, males with a bald head were in fashion.

My immediate supervisor Chief Robby (fifty-three years old). I said
to him, "Let me get your opinion about bald heads, sir." He said, "Yes,
sir, just come in, sir, Staff Sergeant. Anytime". I was doing nothing."

"I am sorry for not knocking first, sir, "I respectfully said. "Chief, your supervisor asked me this morning why Private Homes' had a bald head? I told her, "I" I said, "Okay. "I have to call her in a few minutes, and I don't have a good answer, sir. Help me out here!"

"So send Homes to visit the colonel and let him explain himself." the chief said, "like we have nothing to do on this busy Monday morning."

I asked the chief what the commander was' thinking. He said, "I don't know"."

Private First Class Homes left to go explain himself to the colonel. When I returned to his desk an hour later, he was quietly sitting down there with his famous goofy smile. I said, "Well, what did you tell her?"

He replied, "The commander said to not tell you, she will call down here just as soon as I get back."

When the call came in, Private Ward answered the phone. 'It's the commander, Chief, She wants to talk to you"

Chief waved his hand for me to come near the phone. "We are standing by, madam' Chief said.

The commander stated, "Okay. I've got some satisfying news, guys, about our soon–to-be Specialist Four Homes. "Guys, Private First Class Homes is not a skinhead."

"That is a relief to hear, madam," said the chief. At the same time Chief and I looked at each other and our shoulders went up at the sometime.

---

**Lessons Learned:** If your office is located far away from your employees and you don't visit them frequently, then you can't possibly know them well enough to know their motives. And just like kids, employees will emulate you.

---

Specialist Homes had what I thought was a bad habit of asking me if he could be excused to use the restroom. It started back when he was just a private a year ago. It made me uncomfortable now because Specialist

Homes was a much mature and respectable young man. He would walk or ride his bicycle everywhere he needed to be, he ate only in military dining rooms, he saved his money, and I saw nothing wrong with any of this; I just did not understand why he was so conservative. He was one of my best soldiers, but just a little different in a good kind of a way. But he got on my nerves by asking too often, "Sergeant," "can I go and use the restroom?"

I would always say, "Go-ahead, Private, "and I would think nothing about until he kept on week after week asking me, that same question,; "Can I use the restroom?" One day, I just had had enough. I put a stop to it. "Specialist Homes," you ask me one more time for permission to use the rest-room, and "I will tell you, "No! You cannot go to the restroom.' "You're bugging me out when you ask me this". "Just tell me you're going, and if I am not here, just go!""

He said, "Okay, Serge." "I meant Sergeant"."

On the other hand, Private Ward and the others acted just the opposite, they would say, "I am going to the restroom; be back shortly, Sergeant." I thought they felt comfortable in this workplace.

> **Lesson Learned:** As leaders we have the responsibility of making sure employees are comfortable in their employee roles.

Now I am going to tell you about one more soldier I supervised who I thought was comfortable with decision making in the workplace, nineteen year-old Private Ward.

I thought I was tricking the entire office for my own personal reasons. I had a slick way of taking quick smoke breaks outside the work areas to release some office stress and maybe take a short power nap, thus finding a moment of peace with anybody noticing. The trick was, the two-cap trick.

Nobody but Chief Robby and I smoked, and he was the only other person who knew about the two-cap trick because he taught me. Chief said in Vietnam they tricked each other a lot to disappear from work for short periods of time. In the army a soldier is authorized to have two caps. This is how it works, and maybe you can try this at your workplace.

I walked inside my workplace, where everyone could see my cap on my head. There was a second cap in my trouser cargo pocket. I would leave one cap on my desk when I decided to disappear from the building. When someone came looking for me and did not see me, but saw my cap on my desk, the person would assume that I was somewhere inside or nearby the building. That was the two-cap trick.

When my data-processing clerks were printing the output sheets, one of my senior sergeants would stay and help them with printing, which took about thirty minutes of time, just enough time for me to sneak outside for a short break. I know this was not fair, but this was a time when men abuse their position of between going to and coming back from work. We really thought this was okay.

But it was not okay with Private Ward. Private Ward confronted me and Chief about it, and she struck up a long–overdue conversation that put an end to my two cap tricks.

Private Ward was the youngest female, in 1996, and she had a different view about how their time should be used in the workplace. She was always a concerned person, and improving the workplace was high on her list of necessary changes. I always knew what directions her mind was going in because she sought information from me often.

I thought one of my senior female sergeants would lead the charge for changes in the workplace. But they did not. One day Private Ward approached me and said, "Sergeant, respectfully, why do you and the others take so many smoke breaks during the day?" And we girls don't?"

I said, "What do you mean by that Private Ward?"

She said, "Every hour or so someone in management goes outside for a smoke break or a break, and we females are not taking any breaks."

I said nothing, so she went on to say, "And, Sergeant, you leave your cap on your desk, and then you leave the office for some time."

I said, "Do you smoke"?"

She said, "No, Sergeant,"

So I quickly replied, "Then give yourself a break sometime."

She smiled, and then said, "We really would like to take a hair salon break instead of a regular break."

I said, "How is that?"

"Well, you management guys go and get your haircuts during the workday, and we females can't until the weekend. I am asking you. Sergeant, to allow us females to get our hair done during the weekday at least once every two weeks."

I said. "Would your work be caught up before you walk out of the building going to that hair appointment?"

Private Ward smiled with excitement and said, "Yes"! The other females and I will rotate and take care of each other's customer' stations."

I said, "Okay-deal!"

This is why I promoted Private Ward to specialist, she cared about office improvements. She was going to be a good leader someday. This moment made me think a lot about my two senior females who should have come to me or just implemented these changes themselves. I guess they thought I was not a negotiating type leader. I paid more attention to my employee's' needs.

> **Lesson Learned:** Don't be afraid to huddle with your employees, It can help improve production, and employee and leader relationships. The retail giant Wal-Mart does so every day.

# CHAPTER 8

# The Final Checklist

FINALLY RETIREMENT WAS LESS THAN a year away. I was getting tired of packing up my family and moving them from state to state. My last military job title was Senior Enlisted Adviser. I had responsibility to travel and stay overnights in different New England states to inspect and evaluate the United States Army National Guards and United States Army Reserves Logistics and Supply and their personnel training programs. I checked to see what they were doing wrong and wrote it down and reported it with my fair recommendations to my commander.

My commander was responsible for all the commanders throughout the six New England states, keeping a one-army training concept active. I had a standard two page checklist of things-to-Do and communicate to our army clients, record the outcome of my visits.

My first impression was that my presence made our Army National Guard and Army Reserves clients very nervous, and I was also. On my very next visit in another state, I faxed a copy of my checklist so they could be better prepared for my visit when I arrive on their site. It worked. No more visits with awkward moments trying to stay professional while thinking and looking like soldiers who did not know what they were doing.

Back at our staff office, my coworker and friend Erven, our Human Resource/Junior Staff Sergeant, was having family problems he needed help resolving, but he was afraid to discuss his family problems with his newly assigned supervisor, Sergeant Anderson.

Erven's car and SUV were in the repair shop, I helped him deliver his vehicles to the repair shop. I offered Sergeant Erven rides to work until his car was repaired.

Erven and I were next door neighbors, we were scheduled for a two day business trip to visit a company in Connecticut. On the ride back home, Erven mentioned to me that his wife had a medical appointment, and he didn't know how he was going to take here to her medical appointment with both his vehicles not working.

When we returned home, it was Sunday afternoon, I parked my government commercial vehicle in the apartment underground parking lot and told Erven to use it come Monday to take his wife to the appointment. I made the choice to allow Erven to drive my government vehicle come Monday morning without permission from my executive manager Major Bostic.

I did feel I should have asked my manager for her permission first; however, I was the vehicle dispatching manager. I feel felt I was privileged enough to make my own decision in helping a coworker and friend.

When I got in my office on Monday morning, I extended the use of the car in Sergeant Erven's name for one more day. I waited until after lunch to inform my Major Bostic about what I had just done to help Sergeant Erven and his wife.

After lunch I thought was a good time to talk with Major Bostic. I got yelled at and I deserved it. But then she paused and said, "I would have made that decision to help a coworker in that situation also. "Tell Sergeant Erven to report to me when he returns, and I will inform his boss. Command Sergeant Melvin, later on so Sergeant Erven wont's be in any trouble."

Sergeant Erven and his wife returned in the vehicle with no problems throughout the entire trip. I informed Erven to report to my boss while I sat with his wife. Two minutes later, he came out smiling. Everything was cool for him, but I didn't know what my boss was going to do to me.

Next day Sergeant Erven showed up on time for our group' board game day with enough pizzas for everyone. The officers sat and discussed blue-chip stocks picking, and some played the chess board game. The non-commissioned officers sat or stood up and played dominos.

> **Lesson Learned:** Real-world experiences can't always be taught in classrooms. Sometimes, as leaders we have to make tough decisions that' are not ethical.

**Note:** Through twenty-two years, the army taught me to work hard, take care of my employees, and do for myself.

## CHAPTER 9

# A Soldier's Perspective on Leadership

THE ARMY OBSOLETED FIRST SERGEANT Robert Yates's Position as club manager. Now he assumes the new position of First Sergeant. For years Sergeant Yates did not have to closely supervise soldiers, and that put him a little out of touch with basic soldiering skills. He and I worked that out; he would call me over to his office to rehearse basic military subjects such as drill and ceremonies behind closed doors. He allowed me to take charge of physical training (PT) more often, and we rehearsed (PT) behind his closed doors also.

There were about fifty personnel assigned there. They all were looking for the first sergeant to lead them. Robert knew he had to catch on quickly in managing smart young men and women. He was a likable and fast learner; He understood managing resources. He talked well enough to motivate soldiers into doing their tasks. It seem to me, he would do well as our leader.

First Sergeant Yates said, "Omonte, I am going to fake it until I can make it" until retirement; this army is changing too fast for me."

I was First Sergeant Yates's first counselee. He was nervous, and I was also. I needed a good report to help my career move forward. He started the counseling session by saying, "I want all my non-commissioned officers to understand what my take on leadership is."

His definition of leadership was detailed and very lengthy. He said. "Leadership means to be motivated to perform to the best of your abilities and come together as a disciplined, cohesive team to accomplish the mission". "Correct employees when they are wrong, and take the time to teach at every possible opportunity." "Inspire and develop excellence and motivate those around you with the sprit to achieve and win". "Direct your employees in such a way as to obtain their willing obedience, confidence, respect, and loyal cooperation in order to accomplish the mission". Continue to be a self-starter, and follow these characteristics of a successful leader.' Assertiveness, bearing, coolness under stress, confidence, creativity, decisiveness, empathy or compassion, endurance, flexibility, initiative, integrity, justice, maturity, self-disciplined, self-improvement, a sense of good humor, tact, friendliness, trustworthiness, courteous, kind, cheerful, obedient, brave, clean, and reverent."

He read all of that to me and then asked if I agreed.

I replied, "Sure. Where do I sign and date this new counseling form?

First Sergeant Yates was a team player even though he lacked a few basic soldiering skills; he was honest about it. He was an important link to management, and this is why first sergeants are called Top-dog. He quickly established a high moral program with the right key people who wanted to be in charge and were not afraid of workplace challenges.

> **Lesson Learned:** Act like you know your workplace subjects and know them at all times, or your employees will see your leadership weakness.

## Chapter 10

# Employed in the Civilian Workforce

WHEN MY WIFE AND I decided where to purchase our new home and start our new jobs, I decided to not work for about two months because I was not sure if I was prepared when I left the military to maneuver the job markets. I had no networking strategies. I was not getting job interviews.

After about three weeks I got disgusted and grew a beard and trimmed it close. I stopped wearing the starched white shirts and tie and visited a temporary hiring agency. When I arrived at the temporary hiring agency, it was here that I got my first job after retiring from the military. So I did not give up searching for a new career. I visited one more temporary hiring agency and got hired long enough to obtain a full-time job with the potential to transition into a career. After being sent to work three weeks here and there, the agency called me to come in for an interview for a truck driver job opening.

I applied for a truck driving job delivering a variety of bread products to local grocery stores, fast food restaurants, and sandwich shops.

Working for a temp-agency was good for me; they were kind and professional in finding me many two weeks jobs until they could find me a better-paying job. It felt like a good deal to be driving alone, with no manger micromanaging me.

The first day on the clock at the new job, I was properly introduced to everyone. I felt like I was a very important person (VIP). They were friendly and helpful to me, making me feel welcome in the company.

My immediate supervisor's name was Tyr Roberson. Tyr assigned Anthony Montgomery to Train me until I was fully trained-up to take on full-time responsibilities as a truck driver. Anthony was a great mentor, and he later in life became a great friend and good minister.

I could tell Tyr was an inexperienced supervisor and he liked to delegates responsibilities to others. After three weeks had passed, he had mismanaged his work time somehow; I felt he did not have the respect of the other drivers.

The reason I say this is because he failed to assign a driver to take my route while I was on my mandatory medical appointment for three days. I requested those days off through the main office prior to signing all the hiring documents. If I did not attend this appointment, I would lose out on all my future veterans' medical benefits. I thought my supervisor Tyr would understand my situation because he was a veteran also; I thought this was no problem.

Tyr called my home the night prior to my three days off for the medical appointment. Over the phone he explained to me, "I need you to come in to work tomorrow morning and drive your truck; 'I could not find anybody to take your route."

Immediately I reminded Tyr, "I gave you the appointment letter well in advance one month out to be exact.

He repeated him-self, saying the same thing. I replied, "Okay. "But said I would be at work in three days. I hung up the telephone quietly.

I was happy working as a bread products truck driver, but I began to have second thoughts about having a job when I returned. Over those three days, the phone call between Tyrone and me made me think about getting fired. The office had assured me they liked me because my uncle Jaycee was one of their best employees prior to me arriving.

I returned as I said I would. Tyr did not speak to me that morning. Speaking the greeting of the day was a gesture for everyone in the South to show respect. It also meant respect was given back. Tyr stepped aside twice with no greeting. It was obvious; Tyr was not speaking to me. I just experienced a bad feeling.

That day on my long ride, I heard on the radio, the bad news about the weather turning into ice the next day. Being an experienced snow driver from up north, I believed this was going to be a dangerous ride come tomorrow. This state was not prepared with snow removal equipment like the northern states. That meant trouble for all drivers. That same day, light snow began to fall. That was my sign from God to quit my first job as truck driver and trust in God to make everything all right.

I'd finished my deliveries. The snow had started falling heavier than expected. I made it back from driving to Pylon, across I-20W going to Saluda, When I arrived into the warehouse I parked my truck for the last time. When I left the warehouse, I called Tyr's boss and informed him I was quitting my job as truck driver. I said, "Sir, "this is my two weeks' notice". "This is not what I wanted to do, but this is what I feel I have to do." Tomorrow came, and the roads were very icy and dangerous for long-distance driving.

**Lesson Learned:** Know whom you are dealing with; leaders are never dealt a favorable hand to play. Get to know your employees.

A temps-for hire agency across town assigned me and about fifty other jobseekers to work at MODINE Automotive Production Manufacturing Company. When I reported for work, Kenneth Smith was my immediate supervisor. Kenneth was a retired artillery soldier. He started working at MODINE when the company first started up.

Kenneth said to me, "Omonte ..." "Sir?"

"If you don't mind me asking you this one question? "I want to know why you went through a temporary hiring agency to work for MODINE. Our Human Resources Department would have hired you; they like hiring ex-military people."

I replied by saying, "Thank you, sir". I just got out two months ago, and I did not know I could just walk right into the HR office." I was quite pleased to have a supervisor who would call me by my first name. I said that I did not mind being a temp for a little while".

Kenneth said, "Okay." It won't be long before the company makes you a permanent employee". "Just don't refuse any additional work given to you. Don't be like some of the other temps."

As we were finished working for the day, Kenneth said to me, "You play Lotto?"

I said, "Yes, but you have to drive to Georgia to purchase a ticket."

Kenneth then said, "Let's go; I'll drive." We will be back in one hour."

I said, "Let's go," and we were soon driving on I-77 South to connect on I-20 to Augusta, Georgia. Now I felt like I was a team player again. Riding with the boss. I had a relatable supervisor. Kenneth said his son lived in Louisville, Kentucky, and he drove there about three times a year to visit him.

I smiled and said, "I will ride with you and stay over and go the horse track there or the Derby."

He said, "I like playing the horses also."

I offered to help him drive on the way back from Augusta. As I drove, I said. I notice, a lot of the temps are not coming back to work anymore. What is going on?" He said. "The temps are making too much rework, Costing the company money and time". You start doing that, I've got to fire you. People in those groups are being sent home for good. They refuse to come in and get paid to reduce the rework. They are lazy, and they had to go. They were cited for improper work clothing, exposed tattoos, body piercing, and distracting male/female body parts all reasons why someone will be sent home for good. The real reason is MODINE only needs about forty new full-time workers, and the rest will be let go Say nothing about what I just told you."

Later on, there were rumors around the plant, saying the plant was shutting down. Management had begun a process of eliminating temporary employees to save money. This rumor was true; temps were being released every week for that reason. Kenneth would say "Rework is just scrap," excess scrap!" We can't sell scrap, ladies and gentlemen. Too much rework will get you relieved real quick.

Kenneth asked the remaining groups "who wanted to work the painting booth." No one had any interest in operating the painting booth but me. "I will as long as someone will train me to do the task.

"This job will pay you five dollars per hour more. Say nothing about this," Kenneth said.

I'd heard this before and said nothing to nobody.

"You have to undergo additional drug test screening," and in addition, "can you work one hour overtime each day?""

"I can." I said. "I could use the extra money, and I won't say anything to anybody." I was smiling like a proud new daddy.

Once two months had passed, Kenneth's group was down to fifteen temps. Kenneth told the temps about the company implementing a draw-down to lay off everyone with the exception of a few mission essential people in shipping and receiving. Because I worked fast and took on many additional jobs on the floor that many refused to, the other temps and even a few regular workers would ask me. "Are you full-time now"?"

I said to them, "I am a temp like you."

Four months later, the company laid us all off just before Christmas; we'd known this day was coming. We received our unemployment documents and went home. I went home for good. I had purchased a new truck and continued to find work. Kenneth and the others were called back to work and returned in February or March the next year. Not me; I was working out of state.

> **Lesson Learned:** Promote those who exceed the office standards and demote those who fail at not achieving office goals.

Mr. Whitley was a millionaire entrepreneur who just could not stay away from working. Maybe because, he also was owner and the project manager. For his largest project in some time. It meant millions to be made as every new cell-phone tower is turned on. One year was all I agreed to on my employee contract.

I remember Mr. Whitley an elderly, friendly, quiet gentleman, dressed from head to toe in the latest quality clothing casual or professional. He set a high standard in clothing ware.

Mr. Whitley would fly in and drop in at our offices unannounced all the way from his home in Gardner, Massachusetts. Maine or North Carolina or wherever he thought he needed to be, he flew there.

He would fly in to check on the momentum of the projects, and some-times we would talk to him via weekly conference calls. The man cared about moving projects forward and making money.

I was allowed to sign in weeks early. The new director had to keep me gainfully employed working with other contractors until June. This was phase I, and I would be the expert in phase II in June.

Mr. Whitley did his homework and discovered Human Resources (HR) had forwarded bogus college credentials of employees who' were not qualified to work the positions they interview for. Mr. Whitley had to reprimand the project director for not knowing this information.

I was fully qualified to be onsite, I was locked into a six-month apartment rental just like many others. I signed in to work two months earlier, just like the project director instructed me to. Mr. Whitley visited us in March, He was checking who was on his payroll for the next phases: phase II and III-of this project. I was afraid he was going to send me back home because Mr. Whitley was known for firing his employees and rehiring them.

Since my true assignment was not supposed to start until June (phase II). I kept myself busy every day doing whatever it took to keep busy so I wouldn't get fired.

When 9/11 occurred, Mr. Whitley sent a team to New York to help establish temporary wireless communication services in Trade Center areas. This was a sad day as we all watched the event unfold on our laptops from all over.

An abundance of incoming cell phone calls kept us from working. It was the only reason the project was delayed, and our jobs were spared, except one person. We thought nobody was going to get fired, since the New York City needed our skills.

Mr. Robert Sheldon was one of six Zoning & Permitting survey managers who was not so lucky. I clearly remember him taking me with him on daily business trips to the town halls, looking for local property owners to later make contract deals with face to-face with the healthy incentive of cash or checks. Mr. Sheldon and I were a team until he started taking flights back home to Florida too often and missed too many mandatory business meetings when Mr. Whitley would visit. We were supposed to be finding potential customers who would rent us their land to add or build cell phone towers on.

I was missing my friends and family also, but not enough to miss important meetings. Robert would not stick around for the meetings; he was gone too often, and the director was losing control of him.

Mr. Whitley showed up in the office unannounced early on Wednesday morning. He said, "Big meeting in the morning, guys. 'I need to check the personnel files again." It was time for our first quarterly project progress report meeting. Who was going to brief Mr. Sheldon's portion because he was in the air flying back to Florida again and I had stopped working with him a month earlier.

The next morning, it was time. One by one we briefed what was happening. My portion was the warehouse, and it lasted five minutes.

Mr. Whitley said, "Guys, the project has exceeded my expectations of making millions." "Close up early today; you decide when to close up today. I will see you all on Friday night for dinner" at the Bar-Grill at seven o'clock. Everything is on me."

That night before we had too many drinks, Mr. Whitley said to me, "Monte son, I would have fired you prior to Phase II, you know,"

I replied by saying, "Yes, sir."

He continued to say "Instead, I fired your project director for miss-managing the personnel spending budget at such a critical time". "I am sorry we shifted you around from manager to manager, but phase I was unstable times; "And thank you, son". You did not cause me any trouble like the others did. "I know you took charge when Leroy back home several times to North Carolina". They did not know I knew about that." Good job, son."

I was glad that this project was now sounding like it was ending. Mr. Whitley shook my hand and said, "Sorry for my bad behaviors, "I was just getting things done, son"

I replied by "saying. "I understand, sir." As for Mr. Sheldon, he was fired via Mr. Whitley' cell phone.

**Lesson Learned:** What management expected of us is that we are available for travel without any family issues and have our personal life taken care of prior to when we move on to other projects.

On September 8, 2015 I suffered a brain hemorrhage and almost died. I had recently loss my brother, the finest firefighter I know. His death and my car accident helped me make up my mind to retire from the Government workforce.

I did not know how unhappy I was about my brother's passing away until I wrote a thank-you letter to my coworkers.

The letter goes like this; "I don't remember blacking out. But I did, and I hit a car from the rear. Amazingly I braked in time, causing little damage to both vehicles. The driver I hit, was not hurt. He and I exchanged a few caring words to start the process to contact our auto insurance companies". "Had this accident not occurred that morning when it did, I would have continued to drive onto I-20 Highway.

"That morning at the accident scene, "I remember talking with an emergency persons." The next thing I remember is I was standing in the vehicle right traffic lane. "About the same time, my wife had received an emergency phone call about my accident; it was one of our friends, someone whom we had known since age five. She was my guardian angel that day. Later on at the hospital, I remember thanking her for watching over me.""

When my wife arrived, she started yelling at me to get out of the road. My wife got out of her car and guided me to her car. She said. "I am taking you to the hospital right now"!"

Once I was inside, it was then I passed out again. What I remember next was awakening during an MRI test. I did not know it, but I was being examined. I called out wanting to know "what was going on "! I tried to remove this noisy thing, and quickly I began to fade out.

"This time, I woke up in the hospital room, where my wife and my son were sleeping in the bed next to me". "My son lives in Boston, Massachusetts and I wondered to myself why he was there. 'At that time, I noted that I had a very sore right arm and tubes in both arms." "I knew something was very wrong with me, but I just couldn't figure out what it was.

"When I could not make sense of what was going on, I thought maybe this was my last week in this world. "I prayed and prepared myself for that moment to come. Shortly after I prayed. Pastor Howell and his wife walked in. They immediately prayed for me. "We started to chat for a short minute, and they left and I rested right away. "There was so much that had happened, I could not remember it all. I do remember the food was awful. I refused to eat just about everything, but I drank my coffee and water every day".

"A few days later a doctor introduced himself as my doctor. He said." "Do you remember me?"

I replied by saying, "No, sir."

He smiled and said I could leave the hospital that day and go home, it was one week later. As we were leaving the hospital that morning, I asked my wife what medications I had been given, she replied, that the doctor had not put me on any. I said nothing more; we just continued on and visited the medical records room. My wife signed for my medical records, and then we drove home.

"Being back home, recovering has not been to physically challenging. "What is challenging is waiting to recover". "Waiting for the right time to do something new. "I was twenty pounds lighter, and right now, I feel okay about my weight. "My nurse visited me for two days in one week, and it was decided to end these visits. I was okay with that decision because I felt great. "My relationship with God, and the people in my life is the only reason why I am still living. I thank God for keeping his hands on me. What that means to me is when God has his hands on you, you are going to be going with him or you're going to be doing great things in His name somewhere".

The economy was bad thirteen years ago, or I would never have applied for a government job or career. I would like to say I was part of a team, but I was not. I spent almost thirteen years being a slave to people of power who just wanted things done their way, fair and not so fair. I decided to leave the government workforce to pursue a third career and not be a go-fer for anybody anymore again.

## CHAPTER 11

# Skills and Abilities That Makes Good Leaders

QUALITY CONTROL IN MANAGEMENT IS managing people expecting to accomplish an acceptable level of excellence in the people's performance. If leaders are not training employees, it is because they do not know any better, or they do not care about training until something goes wrong. Together, supervisors and managers are responsible for providing a variety of quality training. There are three skills that a leader should have in order to teach employees effectively:

- *Human Skills:* are the key to having the ability to create an environment that allows employees to feel free to express their ideas and become trained team players and productive employees.
- *Technical Skills:* are the key purpose behind training people. They gives employees the opportunity to learn something new to improve productivity.

- *Conceptual Skills:* are the key tool that enables managers to view the organization as a whole and predict the effects that their actions will have on others before taking such actions.

## After-Action Review (AAR)

An after-action review is an effective way of bringing new solutions to the table for reoccurring project problems so the company can get better at what they do; it, helps change the behaviors to get better results through lessons learned.

If management is not conducting AARs, they are not improving anybody nor making changes to achieve greatness in the workplace. After-action reviews (AAR) allow leaders or staffers and their employee's development opportunities to stretch their creative minds in a formal or informal setting without any repercussions from management. So gather up everyone for a positive, meaningful meeting and discuss what went right and what went wrong and create some new, improved solutions that will work better the next time. Remind employees it's okay to disagree as long as they do it agreeably; also remind them they will not be punished for telling the truth as they see it or understand it

## Conducting Meetings

Always start your meetings on time and conclude the meeting in a timely manner, Impact meetings last about fifteen minutes and end shortly after that. Lectures extend the speaking time of sixty minutes or any time longer will be considered too long. Especially without allowing the employees a break. Taking too long to get to the point often disengages the employees or anyone listening from the learning process, causing information to quickly forgotten. There is not much you can do about impromptu meetings except to attend them and try not to have one. Direct the meeting yourself, and not let the employees take the lead in your meetings.

Before starting your meeting, circulate the agendas in advance to allow employees to prepare their thoughts and any questions they might want to ask you. Always discuss the now, the past, and the future workplace agendas to make it clear an honest attempt has been made to express concern over subjects.

## Conducting a Safety Briefing

It is important to conduct a safety briefing with employees before they leave the building for a holiday weekend. They may not be thinking about safety, just about having a great weekend; they may not be conscious about protecting themselves from themselves, let alone protecting themselves from others. Government and military employees are required to receive safety briefings from their workplace leaders when granted a holiday time off or approved leave. This is a good example for every workforce leader who wants to keep his or her employees informed about being safe.

After the briefing is complete, you're off the hook should the employee gets hurt or killed while not on the job; loved ones will seek compensation for loss of their loved one. Give the employees something to think about; have the employees read, date, and sign their names to a safety memo or letter to show that they're aware and understand the safety briefing's intents. Now the employee will have something to think about over the holidays, it is that serious, and yet some workplace leaders take it for granted, just hoping the employee will return to work without incident.

## Controlling Rumors

It's, your responsibility to try to stop bad rumors. Bad rumors in the workplace create fear, and jealousy; they can tarnish an employee's name and the company's brand.

Talk with your employees or the groups responsible for spreading the bad rumors. Make them provide you a reason why it is so important that they spread bad rumors. Whatever their answers are, seek reprimand actions. There is almost no way to stop rumors from spreading like wildfire except to try to control them to reduce their spread.

## Standing Operating Procedures (SOPs)

A standing operating procedure (SOP) is the same as a standard operating procedures (SOPs). The military prefers to use the term *standing operating procedures* because they govern so many proceedings, more than would be governed in the civilian workforce. Both SOPs are a worker's quality control guide of information that directs the workers to navigate to specific standards; they sets proper expectations and set the consistency vital for business owners that operate companies like pharmacies or manufacturing plants. Customers or business owners would not like it if your employees failed to read and follow the guidelines on how to measure a product like medicine distribution.

Imagine for a minute; a lot can go wrong here because of incompetency, a life can be lost, the company brand could be sued, and the company brand could be tarnished through the media. People will not like it if they call into a business to place a purchase order for a product or get service information and nobody picks-up the office phone. When minutes pass without an answer, the potential customer will simply stop calling; the potential customer will call someone else and go spend their monies elsewhere.

Leaders without a SOP guide, should write their own quality control guide and call it the internal standing operating procedures (ISOP). They should fit your business protocols to keep customers and make you money. If leaders are not checking their employees' ongoing quality of work, they are not managing.

## Violence in the Workplace

Workplace violence may be prevented through good leadership, prior planning, employee involvement training, and utilization of appropriate training resources. When violence happens in the workplace, employees' emotions are disrupted; they are then afraid to be in such a close environment, and the entire daily work schedules can go off track. When that happens, the leader or someone else must get involved to take actions to restore the workplace to normal.

Workplace violence is nonphysical or physical violence or threats against a co-worker or visitors. You will never be able to predict workplace violence or when an act of violence is developing. It is everyone's responsibility to report it if and when it occurs. Instruct the employees not to enter any place where they may feel unsafe. They should inform a manager and continue to seek help. If the situation is really out of control, call law enforcements or emergency responders. Violence in the workplace is a growing concern for many employers and employees, so schedule a class on workplace violence. Don't try to defuse the workplace violence yourself; you may also become a victim unnecessarily.

Would you know what to do if a coworker threatened to harm another coworker? Or harm you? Moreover, would you know what to do if a coworker brought a firearm to work, displayed it, and talked of firing it? Would you know where to run and hide once the shooting started? The active shooters' plans are to operate undetected to hurt or kill everyone in your office, to including you. Their targets are places where people are present; military installations, hotels, public areas, public transportation, and other places they think are of human interest.

The Occupational Safety & Health Administration (OSHA) has information on workplace violence, get it! But unfortunately, there is no sure way to predict when workplace violence is going to occur. Report any suspicious acts that look like a possible threat to you or the community. The military brings training awareness classes to the workplace to help prepare workers for possible attacks.

Workplace violence is reduced or prevented by providing employee involvement training and utilization of appropriate training resources.

## Holidays

September, October, November, December, January, and February are considered stressful months for people all over. Military experts have prepared suicide prevention classes for years around these months. When someone dies, it leaves a personal professional void in the workplace because we cared about that person and depended on that person.

Encourage your leaders to schedule a mandatory suicide awareness class. Not all the warning signs will be present, so never assume that family members or your employees are doing okay; check on them.

Now I will tell you this true suicide story: At about five o'clock in the morning in darkness, the first sergeant began to call out everybody's names to ensure 100 percent accountability of attendees for that morning's physical training (PT) session. Our friend Jim was not there. Nobody knew where he was. We begin a daily PT routine exercises without Jim. At about six-thirty, our group returned from a two mile run. Afterward, we were dismissed to shower, eat breakfast, and go to our assigned jobs. One hour later, we returned to our jobs. There was no sign of Jim. At 8:00 a.m. during the morning platoon sergeant meeting, First Sergeant Benson told me, he went home the day before feeling worried about Jim. First Sergeant Benson said, "I hope for Jim's 'sake he just overslept;" I can forgive him for that." The first sergeant asked Sergeant Jones to go with him to check on Jim before going back to his office. The first sergeant said, "I will call your chief and let her know you are with me this morning." At about nine o'clock, Sergeant Jones and the first sergeant arrived at Jim's house. They rang the doorbell more than once. They knocked hard next to the door several times and realized five minutes later that the door was already open. They both were now sensing something was wrong here. They stepped inside and called Jim's name, walking around and searching the rooms until they found Jim lying dead in his bedroom. In Jim's left hand was a Dear John letter, where his loved one ended their relationship on St. Valentine's Day. In his right hand, Jim was gripping a pistol, with the barrel of the pistol in him mouth. Jim's death was later declared a suicide. No one had known Jim was having personal problems.

The thought of committing suicide may not be in your mind, but someone you know or work with the thought maybe considering committing suicide. Leaders everywhere should always focus on having a suicide prevention training awareness class at some point, hopefully not just after someone taken his or her or her own life.

CHAPTER 12

# Counseling Employees

MAKE SURE YOU ARE COUNSELING your employees. When counseling employees, do it as often as needed, but normally it's done once a year. Select a date and time to counsel the employees, and inform them well in advance. This way the employee has an opportunity to compile workplace information he or she would like to discuss during the counseling session.

Supervisors and managers together they are responsible for evaluating and counseling employees' work performance at least once a year or every three months to correct bad behaviors or reinforce good behaviors. Don't just tell the employees they are doing a great job; put it in writing. Be detailed in your discussion. Decide what information is going to be discussed first. Be fair and allow the employee to speak freely without any repercussions.

Use a performance counseling document with a rating point system, for example: 1 = excellent, 2 = successful, 3 = fully capable, and maybe 4 = marginal performance. Face-to-face is the best way to counsel an employee. Keep a copy of this counseling form, along with notes you wrote or notes the employee may have provided. File it in the employee files until the next counseling session.

A faire and unusual way of conducting personnel counseling is to have employees write an honest statement highlighting their past job performances; don't let them exaggerate too much. It worked years ago, and it still works today. You rewrite these statements to reflect the truth. The employees will feel good about being able to participate in creating their own true performance rating report. It may be a good idea to let them get involved in stretching their minds a bit.

My supervisor Mr. Rubi once said to me, "Momte, we have a lot of junior soldiers to evaluate. Have them write a short statement highlighting their past work performances as they can remember them, and do this until we depart from this assignment. Tell them to keep it honest and not exaggerated. "Let the soldiers know that you will fine-tune their drafts. Make sure they know you will have the last decision on how the report will be drafted" before passing it on to me." The chief then asked me, "Can you remember everything they did?"

I said, "No, sir."

He replied "I can't say I can remember either."

During the next counseling session, the junior soldiers had no problems disagreeing with their reports.

"The chief said, "This is how the executive officers prepare their junior officers for successful performance ratings, and it will work with your junior enlistment soldiers as well."

## Employees' Emergency Leave Requests

Supervisors are responsible for tracking employees' time off, whether it be personal time off, medical time off, earned time off, and more. All leave requests should be handled with a sense of urgency and privacy. Senior managers are responsible for making sure the leave form is returned approved or disapproved. Waiting for an approval or disapproval response should take minutes, not days.

Sometimes employees won't have sufficient leave time accrued for use in emergencies. In this case, initiate an e-mail request for leave donations to help. In the federal job system, this is normally done through the Human Resources Department and DRM Department. Contact the employee later, offer your support, and visit him or her to see how he or she is coping. If the leave request is for death of a family member, along with the other employees deliver a signed sympathy card and flowers and, if time permits attend the funeral. In some cases leaders collect monies and give them to the grieving employee to defray some expenses the employee may have accumulated. When the employee returns to work, welcome him or her back and talk less about his or her crisis or loss to avoid an employee emotional meltdown.

Some managers require an employee to obtain an obituary article to account for their time of absence when returning to work and some managers don't.

## Decision Making

Making decisions is what leaders do. When making decisions to put employees in motion working, ask them if they understand the instructions; make sure they understand what their instructions are. Later do a follow up to see if the instructions are being fully executed. Base all your decision making on sound reasoning and moral principles, not emotional desires or feelings. As leaders, we are not there to make friends with our employees, but to work them consistently, keep them happy, train them thoroughly and equally, and be there for them with more than just their job issues. Better training standards, and better job security will be good reasons for an employee to stay.

## Too Much Time-Off

Too much time-off can be a warning sign that employees are having some trouble managing their personal time, they are abusing time off to keep from being involved in work projects, or they just need a break from work. In manufacturing companies at the end of the year, management will use a past attendance report to show time-off facts as a method to determine which employees will get laid off first or terminated first during times when a company slows down or is reorganizing. Records must show the employees times were absent from work. Keep the report on file because you may have to explain to management about that employee's frequent time offs.

## Inappropriate behaviors in the Workplace

Enforce disciplinary actions against any person who engages in physical or verbal misconduct with someone not willing to entertain such advances. Everyone has the responsibility to report harassment or sexual harassment. The harasser can be someone male or female inside the workplace or outside the workplace committing repeated unwanted acts of touching, e-mailing offensive pictures that are sexual in nature, sex-texting, obscene gestures, and more. These people seeks control over other people. Document their actions and report them to your supervisor or someone in management. You may not be intimidated by these behaviors, but other people are. If you are a leader, schedule a mandatory sexual harassment or sexual assault class to bring awareness to this important subject. Once you have scheduled the employees' classes, start a record of the attendees and reschedule classes for those employees who missed the previous class. Employees should be able to enjoy a working environment free of inappropriate behaviors. Undocumented bad behavior can be denied in a court of law because of no trail of evidence or not enough evidence.

## Occupational Safety & Health Administration (OSHA)

Phone calls frequently come in from concerned people who complain about real environmental issues that your company is causing. Guess who will come to inspect you and possibly shut down your business? For example: Your employees are pouring paint into the water drain systems. The smell of propane and diesel fuel made it into the departments where employees are working at their desks. There are many things leaders allow employees to do wrong without knowing it.

Call the Occupational Safety & Health Administration (OSHA), and schedule a onetime inspection so you can know what it is you should be focusing on in terms of not violating any environmental laws. A violation of workplace safety health rules will be the owner's or leader's fault. With just one complaint from a concerned person, a leaders can be out of a job, the company can be temporarily shut down and fined heavily, and there will be almost no room for appeal. Manufacturing companies certify their employees and require them to read thoroughly enough until they understand the operating Standards each day, that manage the processes to produce quality products.

For an example, consider a case when ties blew out and caught on fire when an airplane landed on the runway. Luckily, no one was killed or injured. This international incident prompted a worldwide investigation that was traced back to the US tire manufacturing company. This investigation determined that the night shift workers made these tires. Someone did not follow the quality control specification rules for checking and correcting the production in an output process for making quality tires. The final inspection person did not do a good job checking for defects before delivering the tires to the shipping department. Tires were loaded up and Shipped to the buyers. Before allowing the employees to start working, they all should have read the standard operating procedures (SOP) or, like manufacturing companies, they should have had a quality control system manual available for employees to read each day before working or training so they could make consistently good, high quality products.

CHAPTER 13

# A Leader's Creed

SUPERVISORS ARE NOT MANAGERS, AND they do not supervise other supervisors; they are representatives of managers to the workers and the workers' spokespeople to management. A supervisor is the most vital part of management's efforts to improve productivity and profitability and maintain the company representation. A manager is responsible for least one supervisor Together the manager and supervisor will enforce polices, set priorities, and respond to higher managers.

Below is a list of principles a leader must develop and use throughout his or her career to become a better, and more effective leader in the workplace:

- I will demonstrate patience and understanding.
- I will make every attempt to understand my supervisors' and employees' motivations, and I will find out if my employees work well with one another.

- I will obey policies, recommend new programs, and promote diversity in my workplace.
- I will not let my emotional intelligence become my disadvantage.
- I won't hesitate to reward or discipline a supervisor or employee when he or she deserves it.
- I will listen to what my supervisors or employees are saying, and I will not write them off.
- I will know all the facts before bringing an employee in for disciplinary actions.
- I will make sure the employee appraisal session is not lengthy and is worth the time employee's time.
- I will improve job performances and remove stressful situations out of my workplace based on what I experience and what my overseers are telling me.
- I will meet or exceed the company's vision and objectives with a desire to lead people to win.
- I will motivate employees into wanting to stay in my company with kindness that works.
- I will stay available to my employees and try to provide them with answers as soon as possible.
- I will know all my supervisors' and employee's' first names, and job descriptions.
- I will delegate responsibilities down but not to over manage them.
- I will try to keep employees with whom I can build a foundation and move the company forward.
- I will remove those employees who won't perform to the standard or replace them to work somewhere else in the company.
- I will not lead employees by threatening them or abusing my powers.

- I will encourage employees to work together with their leaders toward common goals.
- I will propose new leadership and systems to accomplish work that will facilitate achieving the organizational vision.
- I will conduct follow-ups for understanding of actions expected from my teams.
- I will establish and maintain departmental priorities and publish new directives.
- I will be a very loyal follower of my senior managers.
- I will make sure my employees understand what they have to do before they start a task.
- I will train the new employees myself, delegate responsibilities to my team leaders, or appoint an experienced employee, and give him or her the opportunity to train new people.
- I will make my case before taking any employee in for an award or disciplinary action.
- I will seek solutions to my workplace problems from other leaders if needed.
- I will work effectively and efficiently with other supervisors in the organization to know their motivations in order to improve my motivational skills.
- I will motivate employees into wanting to stay in my company.
- I will support all work activities, processes, and procedures that support the company's vision.
- I will learn not to over supervise when managing employees
- Will have a polished image and expect the same of my employees.

## First Month on Your New Job

Usually during your first week after being hired in a leadership position, management will take you around and introduce you. But not always. Go out on your own and meet and greet your employees.

Spend a minute or two honestly chatting with them until they are used to you. Do this once a day to where employees expect your daily visits and conversations. If you fail to make your daily visits, some employees will remind you with a smile that they were looking for you because they are glad to be on your team.

## Conduct Cross-Training

Cross-training is popular in the military workforce, It helps the military conduct business with fewer interruptions, and it helps continue the workflow without missing that absent employee who is assigned to that particular job or project that nobody else is trained to do. If nobody else is trained to take over for that absent employee, then the leader steps in and takes over.

CHAPTER 14

# Building Award Documents

WRITING AND PRESENTING EMPLOYEE AWARDS is what leaders must do. Don't just tell employees they are doing a great work put it in writing, set them down, talk about it, and let them know where they stand. Awards have the most impact on an employee when he or she is caught off guard. Whether it is a small or large group ceremony, formal or informal, be motivated to write your best appreciation letters or birthday letters, to show your gratefulness. Maybe take pictures of day-to-day events at work and place the pictures on the bulletin board so everyone can view them. "Say "Meet the Staff" on it somewhere. Give employees cash bonuses or unexpected time off. Your giving sprit will be reflected with the employees often showing up to work earlier than normal, improve production results, and employee' morale higher than normal.

Inspire employees as to why they are there. Place the awards in their hands in front of coworkers, and do not wait until the employee has moved on to a different company or retired. If you cannot have a few minutes for an award presentation, then personally make a phone call or e-mail that employee and tell him or her you are thankful for his or her job performance. Show your appreciation by displaying the employee accomplishments in the building hallway or on the entrance bulletin board, where everyone can view the employee's achievements. Categorize the awardee's work performance with something like this: Distinguished Volunteer, Employee of the Month, Supervisor of the Month, Manager of the Month, or Hall of Famer, and the dates they achieved the status. We fail as leaders in people management and quality control when we don't spread around enough thank-you gestures. Share credits with the employees as often as time will allow you to, whether formally or informally. Schedule a brief work time-out to present the award. Employees won't mind making up the lost time, and neither should you. Awards have an everlasting positive effect on an employee's state of mind in terms of motivation.

**Five Short Paragraphs Examples to Helps Builds Departure Letters:**

1. I appreciate the support you have shown me during our joint service with _____. I wish you good fortune, and I know that you will continue with the same dedication, Good luck.

2. I want to convey to you my appreciation for your professional assistance. Faced with long hours, shortages in personnel, and demanding work schedules, you performed in the finest manner. It has been a pleasure for me to work and be associated with a person of your caliber.

3. You are recognized and admired for exemplary performance of duty while assigned to the "Fit to Fight Cobras", the best company at Fort Jackson, South Carolina.

4. I can honestly say I never met a more professional and outstanding person than yourself. You're the perfect role model needed for all young professionals, Thank you.

5. It is my obligations to say that we are going to all miss you around here. You have made this company grow beyond the owner's expectations and more. The entire office thanks you and wishes you well as you turn a new page in life.

## Eight Short Paragraphs Examples to Help Create Awards Letters

1. During the period of May 12, 2014, through August 12, 2016, Mr. Bobby Jones demonstrated dedication and sound judgment as he spent many hours helping P & C Department meet its mission' goal to 99 percent, above the company's standard of 95 percent.

2. Mrs. Barbara Frasier demonstrated outstanding leadership and executive abilities in supervising the complex system and diversified operations of RBC programming projects during the time of January 24, 2016, through March 24, 2016.

3. Miss Janette A. Green, this year's number one senior base operator, performed a myriad of successful tasks, providing leadership in critical times when personnel were limited by an abundance of tasks.

4. Captain Laura Taylor's resourceful efforts achieved perfection in all phases of her duties, which resulted in an increased 90 percent operational efficiency rate.

5. Mr. Tom Mitchell, a loyal and determined manager, gave unselfishly of his personal time in order to get the job done. His entire period of service has been marked with high standards of conduct and a willingness to expend his every effort to achieve superior results.

6. Mr. Karl Finney Jr. has done a remarkable job as supervisor of twenty assistants while working on a special project (the Bradley Job). This job required great personal efforts and the ability to

work in an ever-changing environment, which many refused to do.

7. Mrs. Lopez resolved many complex problems, proof of her professional proficiency. Through her leadership, she inspired personnel I who served with her to such an extent that all assigned tasks were consistently performed in an exemplary manner.

8. David Smith's professional knowledge and sound judgment, combined with his ability to work without supervision and his willingness to work beyond normal hours, haves gained him many favorable comments from upper management.

## Seven Short Paragraph Examples that Help Build Thank-You Letters:

1. It is a pleasure to forward the attached laudatory comments of Major Robert D. Carter designating you a distinguished soldier. Such outstanding performance is indeed worthy of this recognition and indicative of your genuine dedication and commitment to excellence. It is a privilege to have you as a member of this command. I would like to add my personal thanks for a job well done. FORCECOM Commander.

2. I commend and designate you a distinguished supervisor for your exemplary performance and dedication to the mission during the period of July 28, 2015, through August 31, 2016. As acting supervisor, you distinguished yourself by efficiently responding to all the organization's requirements in the absence of your superiors. This action resulted in a satisfactory rating during a division support inspection. Post Commanding General.

3. As a member of the DE Processing Team, you replaced and corrected all deficiencies noted on 378 automotive systems and components of combat fighting vehicles. Captain of Engineering

4. Your determination, drive, and attention to details significantly contributed to the on-time delivery of the best possible vehicle fighting system to the soldiers in the fighting zones of the Second Infantry Division. Field Site Officer

5. It is with great pleasure that I commend you for achieving the top Employee of the Month Award, November 30, 2016. Direct Manager

6. I wish to applaud you for your successful completion of the Bradley Project, Thank you. Senior Supervisor.

7. Upon the occasion of my departure, I would like to express my profound appreciation for your loyalty and dedication that you have rendered. First Sergeant

**A Letter of Commendation:**

This type of letter is written and presented to an employee who worked beyond management' expectations.

---

(Military Organizational Letter Head Centered)

Memorandum for the Record

To: Staff Sergeant Eddie Carson

Date:  October 24. 2016

Subject: Letter of Commendation

---

I wish to take this opportunity to speak well of you for your efforts that led to the Material Management Section passing in all ten areas of inspection in the most recent inspection in July 2015.

Passing an XYZ level inspection is a noteworthy achievement in itself. Your achievement in this area is especially commendable because the AB Section you managed was short of qualified personnel and your areas of responsibility were not collocated they were in three different locations.

The results of this inspection clearly demonstrate that your leadership, management, and organizational skills are superior to most peers of your position and experience.

You have clearly contributed to this organizational goal "to be a leader and model for excellence across the entire spectrum of operations and support." Furthermore, your achievement personifies this organization's value of excellence "to be all you can be" and "a hundred things done a little better."

You have my professional and personal commendations for a job extremely well done. Keep up the good work.

*Joe L. Carter Jr.*
Joe L. Carter Jr.
Corneal, USA, Intelligence Corp.

### A Letter of Appreciation:

This type of letter is written for a person who did not complain about the hard work she endured on her day off.

Memorandum for the Record

To: Mrs. Lucy Brown, First Shift Supervisor

Subject: Second Letter of Appreciation

It gives me great pleasure to extend these words of appreciation to you for your recent contributions toward the organization and planning of our first annual fall picnic on Saturday, July 4, 2016

Without your help, our first endeavor at a company party would not have resulted in such a sterling success. In a business it is essential that people be able to work together; it is equally important that they be able to rest and relax together.

Your efforts supported your fellow workers and their families. Again, thank you for your help. I am pleased and proud to have you as a member of my company.

*Ann Marie E. Ambar*
Ann Marie E. Ambar
Senior Manager

## A Birthday Wish Letter:

Present this letter as a formal birthday wish letter, or have the group comment on a birthday card and then present it to the employee.

Date: January 2, 2016

Subject: A Birthday Wish

Dear Ms. Mahoney Rodriguez,

On your birthday, I extend my personal wishes that you have a truly happy birthday. Your morale and welfare are very important to this organization. Therefore, we send you best wishes for a happy birthday and hope that you have many.

Birthdays are often a time for reflection on the past and pondering of the future. I sincerely hope that you're reflections focus on positive accomplishments and that your future plans are designed to fulfill worthwhile, meaningful goals.

Once again, have a happy birthday as you celebrate the gift of life.

Sincerely,

*Christopher O. Stockings*

Christopher O. Stockings
Executive Officer

**A Support Letter:**

Be prepared to write this type of support letter for failed employees or employees who have to move on to a new job opportunity because of family hardships.

From: Mr. Matt Anderson, Teacher

Date: August 15, 2016

Through: Assistant Principal Mrs. Sara Harden, Ph.D. E.Ds.

To: Board of Education' for Approval or Disapproval

Subject: Letter of Recommendation to Hire Mr. Wilbert Pickens

Dear Sir/Madam,

I am requesting that we rehire Mr. Wilbert Pickens as one of our seventh grade teachers. I remind you that Mr. Pickens did superior work in helping our students prepare to pass the annual APTF exams with a 100 present rating.

Mr. Pickens is a true leader, who made some poor choices to use drugs to cope with his failed marriage and divorce. I am also aware that Mr. Pickens has been living in homeless shelters for the past year. He stopped taking drugs in order to live at the homeless shelter. The record shows he has cleaned himself up. He could use this school's help in getting back on his feet.

I ask this board to consider rehiring Mr. Pickens.

*Mr. Daniel Reeves*

Mr. Daniel Reeves Assistant Superintendent

CHAPTER 15

# Military Millennials (Stop Talking Bad about Me!)

IN THE MILITARY, MILLENNIAL SOLDIERS have many things to do. They always have something new to learn for about nine weeks in training. Their spirit to win and be a part of a team is imbedded in their hearts for a lifetime. Whether they like it or not, they will learn something positive out of training. If they decide they want to leave and go home, it will take months to one year for release papers to get approved. Because the military has so many rules, millennials there won't be jumping from job to job like civilian millennials.

People say "The newest generation dominating leadership positions in the workforce is the millennial". "Born 1980ish to 2000). They seek flexibility in work; they are text savvy job jumpers; they are lazy, immature, and selfish; and they want everything now! They prefer communicating via e-mail, they are better educated and more ethnically diverse than most of their leaders who will manage them. To sum it all up, they are a supervisor's nightmare.

From my personal experience working with millennials while they were in army training, I think they are technically smart, sheltered, and creative geniuses in some ways, but they have very little experience in domestic' hard work. You'd better be willing to reward them quickly to keep them employed or interested in employment. Back in the late nineties, skilled workers would quit work for a twenty-five cent raise.

I once was in charge of two military millennial privates. One was a recent college graduate, and the other was a high school graduate. I was these guys' supervisor' for one week. I made a decision to allow talking time to see whom I was working with. It turned out to be a good ideal because they both needed to talk to someone.

Trade work is fading out and is getting harder to find. High-tech industries are emerging quickly, and they need strong technology experienced skilled workers; and computer-savvy people; they need fewer old-school skilled workers. Many of today's unemployed are highly skilled in the old technology of the industrial society of yesterday. Older boomers-generation workers may not be willing to conform to the millennials' ways of doing things and will simply retire. Time has birthed a new mind-set of jobseekers that demand to be respected; they know the millennials, will become the dominant working group in the very near future.

Being the team leader is an important link to management; the team leader is most likely the best candidate to be selected to the supervisor position during an in-house promotion. Team leaders sometimes share responsibilities along with management. They are responsible for developing employees to improve profits and growth. Recognizing good and changing bad behaviors in the workforce will position any company to make profits.

**Lesson Learned:** Millennials do not put up with boring workplace leaders and management, not because they're being immature, but because walking away is better than staying to serve in workplaces where they are not appreciated.

## Chapter 16

# Why Employees will Quit Their Jobs

TALENTED PEOPLE WILL LEAVE FOR a new job because they feel confident they can find a better place to work. Bad management is a good reason why employees will quit their jobs for a better job: better benefits, fairer treatment, more salary, and most of all, better employer employee relationships.

**Negative Things Leaders Say to Their Employees:**

- They tell offensive jokes
- They are required work hours without extra pay.
- They limit decision making to leaders.
- They show favoritism to certain employees.
- They make too many personnel changes.
- They micromanage unnecessarily.
- Leaders grab all the credit.

- They make employees feel unsafe at work.
- They miss-manage employees' time.
- They state, "The mission is first!"
- They state, Get it done, and I don't care who does it!"
- They state, "You screwed up again!"
- They state, "I don't care about it right at this moment!
- They state, "Get your butt over here!"
- They state, "The army did not issue you a wife!"

Many of us feel that management overtasks us too often, especially when we work without an increase in our pay. After completing the extra duties without pay, respectfully let management know how you feel about working the extra duties without extra pay. Remember the hiring contract agreement statement you signed accepting the job? Well, you're responsible for any additional duties assigned to you. Your job description list something to that effects. In the business world, that statement is called "scratch my back," and by employees it's called "getting the short of the stick."

## Giving Employee Feedback

It is disrespectful to employees when leaders pretend they are listening to their employees but they are not listening because, their minds are focused on other things, wandering too fast to hear what the employees are saying in the midst of so much going on in the workplace. Slow down if you are in this situation, and immediately refocus on that employee, provide eye to eye contact with that employee, keep the conversation going with eye blinking, saying something like, and "go on." Slowly nod your head or say, "Okay"; this will encourage the employee to continue to talk. You should be catching on to the conversation as the employee express his or her feelings to you. As the conversation is coming to an end, recap the conversation with that employee to gather your thoughts and prepare an honest reply. You don't want to write that employee off; his or her concerns could be just that important. Say, "Let me see if I heard what you were saying." then restate the employ's major concerns. If you're wrong, the employee will realizes you are busy and won't mind helping you recap the entire conversation because he or she wants your answer. Do not write off employees for whatever reasons; they deserve an honest response. Give factual and objective answers because employees will hold you accountable to your every word, and they all may have valuable points to make.

## Staying Late after Work

Don't be afraid to say your employees, "Listen up,
"Go home! "That work will be there tomorrow"." Staying late after work could mean your employees is stressing over undone work because, he or she mismanaged their workload and failed to complete it in the set time allocated.

## Smart Leader Style (Everyone Wins)

Smart leaders are special leaders; they are leaders who have formal and non-formal education, and they can connect very well with most people. They encourage and implement positive workplace changes. They ensure diversity in their workplaces. Smart leaders have a sense of ownership to lead and share with their employees' setbacks and celebrate victory with them. God gifted all leaders differently; some leaders are born with natural relatable leadership abilities, and others are not so lucky. Leadership is the art of influencing people to do something without confusion.

## Authoritarian Leadership Style

Only mature employees will take this type of communication well. The authoritarian leadership style requires a leader to tell employees what to do without getting their advice. There is no time for one-on-one teaching, just direct communicating. Use the authoritarian leadership style only on rare occasions, use Authoritarian Leadership Style

As little as possible, and only when circumstances demand this type of leadership style.

## Democratic Leadership Style

Most of your employees will favor the democratic leadership style because it gives them the opportunity to participate in office decision making. Employees get an opportunity to develop their management skills at the sometime employees feel respected fully aware they are not making the final decision. The employees gain a sense of being valuable team players, assuring them job security. Every employee likes to feel valuable to his or her employer.

## Where Does Leadership Starts?

I believe leadership starts with becoming a good listener and follower, and thus being a loyal contributor to a cause that helps everyone achieve and win. When I was a young soldier ready to advance to the rank of sergeant, my senior leader was preparing me for a promotion competition. He asked me, "What is leadership?"

I responded, "I don't know, Sergeant."

He said "Leadership is the art of influencing, and directing others into accomplishing a mission with less confusion."

When you ask this question today; what is leadership?" you will get many different answers, but the answers will have the same meaning, whether they are short or long definitions. For example: The <u>US</u> military definition of leadership, according to Army Field Manual 22-100 dated: 1983 is: "A leader must provide direction, implements, and motivates. Set goals, solve problems, make solid decisions, and set time aside for planning." If you're in a working position that requires you to direct the activity of others, you're likely a team leader, supervisor, or manager, or you are becoming one. The more a person is educated, gains real-world experiences, and executes good leadership skills, managing the workplace becomes much easier.

**Lesson Learned:** Talented workers will leave the workplace seeking to find newer jobs or career opportunities.

## CHAPTER 17

# Having a College Degree

HAVING A COLLEGE DEGREE MEANS that with the education you learned to get that degree or degrees, you will have a big leg up on most of your competition, and doors will open for you to get a job or a career, depending on which career direction you take and who you interview with. Let's face it; it is a battle to find your place in the workforce after college. When searching for employment, you have to be ready to contend with millions of active jobseekers, not counting the ones that are drawing unemployment and not trying to get back in the workforce. When they do start looking for employment, it can lessen your chances of securing employment.

Your biggest competitors are military jobseekers. Many employers seek former military personnel because of their solid reputation for technical know-how, hard work ethics, and mental toughness, rather than being someone who requires additional training.

A recent college graduate jobseeker's chances are very good to find employment once he or she figures out the next move to get a better job or career, because the recent college graduate should still be in the learning state of mind, capable of easily being train.

If you don't get hired right away, then take a chance at searching the big companies for employment, the ones that pay you while you attend their management training programs while you work. It is a good way to gain real world experience, and this way you secure a job or a career. Those graduates who fail to get hired sometimes return back to college for fear of not being qualified enough in the workforce; indeed, in some cases, it's a good idea to get more education.

My best advice to help any seeker find employment is to try searching the hidden job market. That's not the traditional way of job hunting. The hidden job market refers to those companies that are not advertising their job openings. It is a big challenge to navigate the hidden job market because it is everywhere; there is no wrong or right way to get started.

Hiring professionals are looking for exceptional people, hardworking people, creative people who can bring new knowledge to their workplace. People who have a sufficient level of work ethics. They want someone who can quickly develop professionally, build work relationships, analyze work data, pursue continuous learning, communicate persuasively, manage projects, and have a polished image. Moreover, the hiring authority wants those who can make them money, rather than someone who may run up the training cost budget.

Find companies that are committed to life learning and focusing on leadership and promotion from within. The big retail company Wal-Mart, offers a degree in management training programs. It offers employees the opportunity to learn and grow within their companies. Recent college graduate are especially valuable, because their minds are still in learning mode, capable of assuming management trainee positions, junior supervisor, and manager positions. Also, you can try seeking employment at financial institutions like banks, credit union are one of the first places students find their first employment.

A caring parent I know, wants his three kids to have the advantage of having a college degree or degrees when looking for employment. He expects his children to work hard and earn an education and career, not just a job like he did when a teenager. He said, "I will have the final say on my kid's' education and career selection". "I want my kids to have the best education and jobs opportunities" out there". "I am paying for their higher education, not them. "Think about it;" you and I had many jobs before we had a career. "I highly encourage them to select respectable degrees that pay good money. Like; engineering, academics, nursing, doctor, IT, or any degree field that will pay them three times or more above the minimum wage rate. "Home-boy", all of them will attend a university or join the military like you did. "If they do not succeed, they are going to get out of my house and join any military". Partner, I want to give my kids a better career opportunity than what I had."

> **Note:** Good character and a good first impression are good keys to gaining employment and becoming a successful professional in any workforce industry.

CHAPTER 18

# Know you're Worth before Going to a Job Interview

LEADING UP TO YOUR JOB interview, know your worth before you reach the interview room. During the interview the prospective employer does not need to know your salary expectation up front. Introduce your salary range after you have been offered the job. Don't try to force a favorable salary decision, and don't walk away from an offer, instead, negotiate it until it is reasonable by asking, "Are there any salary increases in the future for me"?" Workforce industries may pay you more based on your maturity, qualifications, experience, and interview performance.

We don't know for sure how much students learn in college and how their degrees translate into value. So we assume their salary should be above the average worker's salary. But that is not always so. When I worked in a manufacturing company, there were many recent college graduates from different universities and community colleges laboring for the same minimum wages. The economy will sometimes dictate your salary coming straight out of high school or college, but you can expect your salary or hourly wages to be somewhere near the dollar amounts listed below.

**First Timers' Potential Salary Chart (my opinion only):**
$25,000–$45,000 with an associate degree,
$35,000–$50,000 with a bachelor's degree,
$45,000–$80,000 with a master's degree,
$60,000–$95,000 with a Ph.D.

No matter how many degrees you have, a hiring manager or authority will attempt to hire you the least amount possible. You won't know it until after you have been hired.

Once you are hired, you are worth more. You will become even more valuable because of your degree or degrees; along with the experience you will gain. Do not pass up and opportunity to gain real experience; it generates value and interest in you. Give your employer one or two years of your time before deciding to quit and move on to a job or career that seems more promising.

## Group Interviewing

A group interview sometimes indicates that everyone in a key position is interested in you. They all want to be a part of your interviewing and hiring process. In this case, your prospective employer may want to escort you around to meet the others to see if your chemistry really matches theirs' at this time you're under the microscope, and he or she is sizing you up to later get input from the key players you just met. If you must ask questions during your interview, ask an intelligent question like, "What changes will occur after I am hired," and how will the changes affect me?", or "What are my additional duties?" "Watch to see who answers first, and figure out if their answers were delivered genuinely. Now you will have just interviewed them.

## A Dishonest Job Interview (a True Story)

In 999, Eddie Foster drove his company bread truck to a job interview across town because he was tired of driving bread trucks, "it was time to change jobs. was time to change jobs". See Eddie landed himself a manager job opportunity interview with Car Quest.

Early that morning, Eddie put his interviewing shoes and clothing on his bread truck. While he was driving his route, the interview phone call came in. The time was set for three o'clock very close to quitting time. Eddie was so desperate and serious about getting that new job, he finished his route super early that day and drove straight to the interview in the company's truck.

On his way to the job interview, he was so focused driving his truck, he did not recognize his wife Annette right away driving in the same direction side by side in the adjacent car lane.

Once Eddie arrived at Car Quest, he drove around back and quickly changed out of his bread product uniform and into his suit and tie and shiny shoes. He walked out from the back of the building into the front, entered the office, and signed himself in for the three o'clock interview. Eddie began introducing himself and started falling-out the ethics questionnaire. Now it was time to sit and get to know the hiring manager. Eddie was very interesting to Mr. Burch, the hiring authority. Mr. Burch escorted Eddie to meet the workers to see what their reactions would be about hiring Eddie as the new hired manager. They all talked for a short while, explaining the day-to-day operation to Eddie. Eddie and Mr. Burch verbally agreed on a decent salary and confirmed a good start date.

After the interview was over, Mr. Burch wanted to see Eddie out the door, but Eddie refused Mr. Burch's offer to escort him. "I can find my own way out." Eddie said "firmly shook Mr. Burch's hand, and left the building quickly.

Eddie walked room the back of the building, he drove right past Mr. Burch, who was standing there waiting to see what vehicle Eddie was going to drive off in.

After all that effort, Eddie never got that phone call from Mr. Burch. One of the questions on the ethics questionnaire read," 'Would you use company property for your personal benefits?" "And Eddie had marked the box that said no.

CHAPTER 19

# How to Build a Smart Résumé for Potential Managers

THE KEY TO WRITING A smart résumé is to arrange your résumé to highlight things that matter to the reader who is deciding whether to pass your résumé to the hiring authority. I am saying this because I did not have to have a résumé until twenty-two years later in my working life, and job hunting was very competitive then as it is now. This chapter will give you the edge on writing an effective résumé to hopefully land a career.

### You're Personal Contact Information:

Make sure the contract information is your current address, e-mail, home: phone number, mobile number, and any web addresses you have that link to a professional profile.

**Replace that Blue E-Mail address with a Black E-Mail Address**

> Ms. Danica Adam-Brown
>
> 75918 Briella Lane, Apt. 5, Charlotte, NC XXXXX
>
> Cellular: (803) 356-6489 or E-mail: <u>ms.dbarker@aol.</u>
>
> <u>com</u> [blue]

1. Place contact information at the top of the résumé.
2. Use your cursor to highlight the underlined e-mail, locate <u>U</u> in the font box, and click on it until the underline under line e-mail address goes away. The e-mail address itself will still be blue.
3. Highlight the e-mail again, locate the color font in the font box, and click on the down triangle to drop down the various colors; click on black, the blue e-mail address will change to a black e-mail address.
4. If you do not make this change, the blue e-mail address will be an eyesore for the reader. More than likely, in the first fraction of a second, your résumé will go south.

**The Objective:**
1. Make sure your objective matches up exactly with the position you are applying for!
2. When you are applying for a job at several companies, you should create a different objective for each job.
3. The objective statement tells the employer what job the applicant is seeking to obtain.
4. Write a short one or two line objective statement giving the employer your sense of a clear direction.
5. The objective is listed above the profile or work experience.
6. Especially use the objective when you are re-entering the workforce.

**The Wrong Way:** To work with an organization where I can continuously learn in the pursuit of achieving excellence, thus getting maximum job satisfaction and optimum career growth. Effectively demonstrate my interpersonal communication skills in a professional environment with the opportunity for growth and advancement. (This is way too long; you're going to talk yourself out of a job)

**The Right Way:** Seeking to obtain a challenging Manager Position (Announcement Number 1Hq07778).

**Profile# 1**

Multitalented, energetic, people driven Human Resource (HR) professional with twenty-five years of insightful experience in recruitment and administration, labor laws, and human relationships. Work well independently or as a team player; effectively manage people with flexibility in multicultural setting.

**Profile # 2**

Extremely resourceful and enthusiastic, make a strong effort to be part of the solutions, and very eager to learn new skills and expand professionally.

**Note:** Use three to four sentences or bullet points that highlight your strengths and experiences. List the profile below the objective. The profile tells who is coming to be interviewed so the interviewer can tailor his or her questions to the jobseeker.

**Core Value or Qualifications:**

In this section, list Six (6) to Nine (9) one or two-word phrases that say a lot about you, the jobseeker; you should not have any problem expressing yourself. This gives the interviewer additional focus on some more questions he or she will be tempted to ask you.

**Experience (in Paragraph Form):**
Lash Group, Charlotte, NC, 01/2013 - Present
Specialist II
Review and verify insurance applicants; benefits and communicate project coverage details to provider. Make sure all questions have been answered. Process requests for product shipments as needed, and review and process requests for patient assistance programs. Provide the highest level of customer service and responsive follow-up services.

**Paragraph-From Notes:**
List your experiences in reverse chronological order; most resent, second most resent, third, and so on. Explain how your achievement help save your company money. Keep your sentences short; no more than three (3) to four (4) lines long. Use six (6) to ten (10) lines if your experience is extensive. Be honest, and concentrate on and recount your achievements, not only your responsibilities. Be consistent throughout your résumé when using bullets from sentences, keeping them four (4) to six (6) lines long. Make sure your paragraphs are short and no more than six (6) lines unless your experience is extensive.

**Experience: (in Bullet Forms)**
Internship Paralegal, 08/2003 - 05/2004
Samuel B. Ingra, Attorney at Law, Dillon, SC

- Coordinated multifaceted office functions encompassing court calendar management.
- Handled administration work with urgency and maintained confidentiality.

- Exhibited excellent organizational and time management skills well as outstanding writing, editing, research, and proofing skills.

**Bullet-Forms Note:**

Use as many bullets as are needed. There (3) lengthy bullets is enough to expand on what you have done for one company. Leave plenty of white space throughout the résumé. Start by using a verb or action word, and use the past tense to explain what was achieved back then.

**Date Notes:**

When writing the date, it is best to use a format that gives the full date, for example: 07/07/2014. Giving the full date makes it clear how long the job seeker has worked. Place the date on the same line to the left or right side of the position and location.

**Computer Skills or Technical Skills:**

Proficient in Microsoft Office: Words, Excel, PowerPoint, Access, and Outlook. Devices: fax machines, photocopiers, e-mail scanners, RF scanners, and other office equipment and devices. Knowledgeable in Adobe Applications, computer languages and scripts; and operating systems, include any certifications you have as technical experience. Specialized in financial software applications. (Computer skills can be placed anywhere on the résumé.)

**Education and Training:**

A recent college graduate should place his or her degree or degrees near the top but below the objective. Place education at the bottom of the last page if you're not a recent graduate.

Brown University, WA
Bachelor's degree in Business Administration

Expected 04/2010
Magna cum laude

Associate's degree in Respiratory Care, Everest Institute, Columbia, SC
06/1999 GPA: 4.00

Ensure all information is current, accurate, and to the point. Failure to provide all your education information on your résumé may result in an ineligible rating. Résumé writers will argue résumés are not complete without a cover letter to get an interview, but I say cover letters are not always required.

## CHAPTER 20

# Four Types of Résumés for Managers Seeking Employment

THE NEXT FOUR (4) EXAMPLES are really no secret; they have been around for years, and are the best examples how to write a résumé seeking a management position. These résumés are designed to persuade the interviewer to submit your résumé to the hiring authority. When you gain some work experience, you should start looking for these four résumés even if you are not a potential team leader, supervisor, manager or executive.

All Generation X employees, should have gained lots of leadership skills by now. Every hiring manager wants someone who can lead people. Below are what leaders' résumés will look like after completing several years of work.

First is *chronological résumé*: it lists all your work experience by dates in a reverse order. In other words, your current job is listed first at the top and then you work all the way back to your very first job at the bottom. This résumé is normally widely used, by people who are career oriented and have considerable experience.

Mrs. Cynthia Brown
302 Oaks Tree Drive, Ayer, MA XXXXX
E-mail: CXY@gogo.com | LinkedIn Member.com

**Objective:** Seeking to obtain a challenging security surveillance officer position.

**Profile:** Disciplined, well organized, highly motivated self-starter; professional with over fourteen years of experience in security protection.

**Professional Experience:**
Training Support Center, Deveins, 4 Lexington St., Ayer, MA
Supply Adviser (Full-Time 06 - 2009 to 05 - 2013
Briefed safety policies; coordinated overnight visit arrangements for military police training support advisers; found time to advise, coach, and evaluate US Army Reserves' and Army National Guard's safety, weapons, first aids, physical training programs throughout the six New England states.

First Security Services 12 - 2007 to 05 - 2009
40 Church Street

Maintained 100 percent security control for two major companies (SONOCO and Gillette Light Industrials). Made sure vehicle traffic, parking, and personnel entering and leaving facilities were being monitored. Safeguarded two hundred working personnel by way of closed circuit television, walking patrol, and driving to outer zones checking property and equipment warehouses. Checked three gate guards and communicated with the Massachusetts State Police to confirm activity and safety. Worked on night shift for three years.

Security Officer (Part-Time) 05 - 2003 to 10 - 2007
D. B. Kelly Associates, Inc., 7 St., Gardner, MA
Stood guard at the Holiday Inn and NASOYA Foods Production Plant. Maintained radio dispatcher duties that required administrative tasks. Read and interpreted new regulations, conveyed clear communication to three team players and enforced safety policies. Worked on an eight hour weekend shift for one year.

Security Guard (Part-Time) 08 -1983 to 05 - 2003
Effectively patrolled and inspected government property against illegally activity.

**Computer Skills:** Proficient with Microsoft Word and Excel; Strong understanding of radio devices and dispatching systems.

**Education:**
Regent College, Albany, New York 04 - 1999
Received BA/Business Administration GPA 3.0

---

Below is *functional résumé*; it draws more attention to the job seeker's work experience rather than the work history. This type of résumé is used when people switch careers often. It can helps hide gaps in employment history and the fact the candidate has been out of work for some time. One disadvantage: is it takes the employer longer to read.

Mr. Nathaniel Jackson

Twenty-Ninth Street, Columbia, SC, XXXXX (XXX) XXX-XXXX

or E-mail: Nja6034256@gmail.com

**OBJECTIVE:** Seeking to obtain a challenging manufacturing production supervisor position.

**PROFILE:** Multitalented professional, instrumental in fabric blending and turning, willing to relocate with company if asked. Without supervision, maintained pocket notes to ensure scheduled work was not overlooked and was completed ahead of production schedules. Handled ordering supplies, shipping and receiving, document preparations. Skilled at MS Word; with medium skill of operating office computers.

**STRENGHTHS INCLUDE:**
- Leadership
- Team Player
- Dependable
- Problem Solver
- Analytical
- Computer Literate

**WORK HISTORY:**

Production Fabric Manufacturing

Olympia Mill, Oakland, CA, 06/05/10 to 12/05/13

Grocery Bagger, Commissary, 12/01/06 to 01/05/07

Fort Bliss, TX

Custodian, Satchel Ford, 11/15/89 to 11/01/04
Elementary School, District 5, Columbia, SC

Production Operator, 06/30/68 to 07/01/78
Owen Mills Inc., Columbia, SC

**EDUCATION:**
High School, Hopkins, South Carolina received Diploma (B Student 05/30/1968)

Available for Employment: January 04, 2017

Below is a *target résumé (military to civilian résumé)*, normally used by recent college graduates seeking supervisory and management positions (a two page résumé). Such a person is highly skilled in one field only and rarely crosses over to another field.

**PAGE 1**

Mrs. Jackie James, USA E-8
123 Hartsville Drive, KY XXXX-XXXX
E-mail: 101jj@got.mail

**CONTINUING EDUCATION:**
MBA Procurement and Acquisition | Webster University, SC | (Expected) 12/2016
BA Interdisciplinary Studies| University of SC |
05/30/2012
AA General Studies | Regent College, Albany, New York, 05/28/2009

**OBJECTIVE:** Seeking a challenging supervisor position with a leading government defense contracting agency.

**CAREER HIGHLIGHTS:**

- Served as the Accountability Officer of Class Supply Support Activity, with 3,071 line items (LINs) worth $12.5 million.

- Maintained an active Secret Security Clearance, with the ability to obtain Top Secret Clearance again.

- Recipient of multiples awards and medals for outstanding achievements.

- Effectively leverage writing expertise to communicate orally and in writing in concise and easy-to-understand summaries of activities.

- Provided positive learning environment that mentored over eight-nine warrant officer candidates. Several candidates achieved academic excellence; two distinguished honor graduates, one honor graduate, and several commandants.

**UNITED STATES ARMY (VARIOUS ASSIGNMENTS) 05/1977 To 06/1999**

Senior Supply & Logistics Adviser (3 years)
Third Training Support Center, Fort Deveins, MA

Automated Logistical Coordinator (5 years)
101$^{st}$ AA Assault Infantry Division, Fort Campbell, KY

Material Control and Accounting Specialist (1 year)
Second Infantry Division, Republic of South Korea

Unit Supply Support Technician (3 years)
Ninth Infantry Division, Logistics & Transportation Division, Fort Lewis, WA

**TECHNICAL SKILLS:** Microsoft Office; Advanced MS Word, MS PowerPoint, MS Access, MS Outlook, microcomputers, typewriters, adding machines, copiers, microfiche files reader, calculators, military accounting systems; standard property book, and a strong understanding of DPAS, PEBUS-E, and ACCESS, GFIBS financial systems.

**PAGE 2**

Mrs. Jackie James, USA E-8
123 Hartsville Drive, KY XXXXX
E-mail: 101jj@got.mail

## Special Qualifications:

- K Logistics non-combination Officer Training / 1997 to- Present

- Corporate government credit card holder ($0000.00) Inactive / 1998 to- Present

- Super government credit cardholder ($1,000,00) Active / 1997 to- 1998

- Regular government credit cardholder ($30 to $60,000) / 1996 to- 1997

**Skills and Abilities:**

- Effective counselor, mentor, and teacher

- Performed complex manual and automated research

- Ability to lead multitasking and put mission first before personal needs

- Presented noteworthy improvement opportunities and willing to learn new ideas

- Excellent interpersonal and presentation skills

**Management Style:** Resourceful, walk around paying attention with all senses for problems; be seen, and talk to everyone who is seen. Work with the people responsible in a positive way to solve problems, focus on positive performances, and demonstrate immediate appreciation.

**Supervisory Style:** Not afraid to interface with clients and staff members to exceed enlistment goals for the United States Army. Self-disciplined, fast learner, perform tasks in a timely fashion, excellent written ability, a skillful oral communicator and have a positive attitude.

**Education Council (Credit Recommendation from American)**
Security Analysts, (6), Supply Chain Management (6), Record Information (3), Bookkeeping (3), Clerical Procedures (3), Computer Applications (3), Field Experience in Management (6), Administration, (3), Military Science (3), Economics I & II (9), Math I & II (6), Hazmat (2), Material Handler (6)

**Related Civilian Occupation**
Audit Clerk (DOT 210.382-010), Procurement Clerk (DOT 249.367-066), First-Line Supervisor (OES 51002), Inventory Clerk (DOT 222.387-026), Material Clerk (DOT 222.387-034), Purchasing Agent (DOT 162.157-034), Shipping-and-Receiving Supervisor (DOT 222.137-030), Warehouse Supervisor (DOT 929.137-002), and Stock Supervisor (DOT 222.137-034).

**Military Leadership Schools:**
ANCO, BNCOC, 88M Phase I & II, 63J, and PLDC Courses: Phases I/II of BNCOC, DOD Hazmat, Basic Recruiter, and Equipment Repair.

**Affiliations:**

- Golf Semi-Pro America Team | 1999 to Present

- Canton Telecommunications Professionals | 2012 to 2015

- Hartford Geek Computer Repair Team | 2011 to 2012

- All Army National Racket Ball Team | 2007 to 2008

Below is a *combination résumé*: it's widely used by retired military and contractors job seekers. This résumé can be up to six pages long to include both the chronological and functional résumés. It begins with the functional résumé format and finishes in the chronological résumé format. It will be difficult because of many facts to write, and it becomes more complex. However, it is a good choice for people with lots of experience.

---

Mr. Harold Caldwell

83 Cottontail Drive, Bing, CA XXXXX

Home: (XXX) 699-9546 or Mobile (XXX) 216-0001

**Objective:** Seeking to obtain a challenging Manager Law Enforcement Position at College City, County, Federal, or State.

**Professional Profile:** Accomplished multifaceted United States Army and Civilian Law Enforcement Officer with thirty–five years of combined experience, committed to excellence. A recipient of multiple military awards and medals.

**Military and Civilian Milestones:**

- Received the Governor David M. Beasley Award 1998 - 2002.

- Highly decorated, organized, dedicated team player with positive attitude to confront disgruntled people in the general public and resolve their situations peacefully.
- Recognized as ambitious outgoing reliable and mission oriented professional.

---

- Well demonstrated abilities throughout military and civilian law enforcement business.

- Criminal Response Teams four (4) years' experience.

- Team player in assisting Investigating Units (IU).

- Seek and establish solid illegal gambling operation cases.

- Seized a large sum of U.S. currency as well as two deportations that held in court a grand jury.

- Trained FTO associated with the Big Brothers Big Sisters program.

- Trained over one thousand new police officers with the South Carolina Police Department.

- Seized three vehicles, arrested for possession, and distribution of cocaine and prostitution.

- As first sergeant, provided leadership and life lasting lessons to subordinates that increased morale and raised productivity levels to exceed the norm year.

- Supervised four senior personnel responsible for safekeeping high dollar valued government property.

- Managed the annual operating budget, monitored quality of life programs for soldiers and family members.

- Participated in security training programs with multinational coalition forces in Iraq.

**Leadership Style:** Straightforward and honest while practicing beliefs of integrity as well as enforcing it. Thrive on challenging tasks like training military professionals and young and new police professionals. Regularly communicate with officers and their families to ensure their safety and well-being. Always provide the proper guidance in the most challenging times under pressure to ensure mission success.

**Professional Employment History:**

Police Officer      1999 - 2013
Columbia City Police Department

Campus Police      1997 - 1999
Benedict College (Private)

Corrections Officer     1986 - 1997
Department of Corrections

**United States Army Senior Leadership Positions:**

First Sergeant, TRN Company, E-8  1986 - 1986
Schweinfurt, Germany

Senior Platoon, E-7 (P)    1983 - 1986
Twenty-Fourth Infantry Division
Senior Food Service Sergeant, E-6 (P)  1980 - 1983
Seventh United States Army and Europe Command

**Personal and Self-Management Skills:**

- Proofreading and document preparation including manual system document filing.

- Assessed and evaluated group leaders' strengths and weaknesses and made positive changes.

- Comfortable in working in arenas with rapidly changing responsibilities.

- Safeguarded and ensured proper functions and handling of all vehicles and weapons assigned.

**Skills and Abilities:**

Self-directed, with good decision making. Handle private information in a discreet and professional manner and avoid compromising a questionable person's privacy.

**Continuing Education:**
Bloomfield College, Bloomfield, NJ 1975 to- 1976 Accounting #I
Central Texas College, Germany 1982 -to 1983
Criminal Justice

Midland Technical College, Columbia, SC | Dealing Effectively with Difficult People and Situations December 15, 2010 (0.30 CEUS)

Communicating Effectively for Positive Community Relations | April 17, 2009 (0.7 CEUS)

Education in Emergency Management (FEMA): Independent study EMI Course August 7 2011 (0.3 IACETCEU)

High school: Newark East Side, Newark Diploma 1974

**Awards, Training Letters & Certifications:**

- Emergency Management Institute | Certificate of Achievement |August 7, 2011

- State of South Carolina Department of Public Safety | Permit to Perform Breath Alcohol Test | January 10, 2007

- City of Columbia, SC | Certificate of Achievement. Street Sweep Responses | Presented May 1, 2006

- Criminal Justice Academy Division | Certificate of Award | July 26, 2005

- John E. Reid and Associates, Chicago, Illinois, | Street Crimes Course | April 1113, 2005

- Carolina Institute for Community Policing | Applied Community Problem Solving | January 28, 2005

- Carolina Institute for Community Policing | January 27, 2005

- South Carolina Department of Public Safety | Police Traffic Speed Enforcement Radar Operator| January 11, 2005

- Multi-jurisdictional Counter Drugs Task Force Training | Criminal Street Gangs II | August 23August 24, 2004

- First Responders: Psychiatric Emergencies Training | Certificate of Completion |January 12 3, 2004

- The MOYE Company | Letter of Appreciation | July 18, 2004 August 18, 2004

- Columbia Police Department | Letter of Commendation |January 9, 2004

- The South Carolina Department of Public Safety Criminal Justice Academy Division | December 4, 2002

- Columbia Police Department Crime Scene Investigations Unit | Certification of Completion,| Basic Fingerprint Collection | December 3, 2002

- The South Carolina Department of Public Safety Criminal Justice Academy Division | September 3 5, 2002

- Columbia Police Department | FAA Law Enforcement Flying Armed | August 8, 2002

- Certification of Training | Law Enforcement to WMD Incidents | April 30, 2002

- Columbia Police Department | Certificate of Commendation | March 23, 2000

- Certificate Department of Defense Army, The United States Disciplinary Barracks Pre-Service Class #08-93/ Eighty Hours Training | August 213 1993

- Seventh Army Training Command Military Community Youth Services | Certificate of Appreciation | January 22, 1993 March 7, 1993

- Youth Services Community Program | Certification of Achievement, Volunteer Services

- Certificate of Appreciation| Moral Welfare and Recreation | September 9, 1900une 06, 1991

Community Life Program |Volunteer Services, Softball League" | July 21, 1981

## CHAPTER 21

# Cover Letters and a Couple of True Stories

Date: December 12, 2017

To: HR Professional

Position: Supply Management Analyst Specialist Announcement number: AFPCMEDDH-527572-0665.

Dear Mr. Allen Jones,

I am a prior army service member. I received an honorable discharge and many awards for my outstanding commitment to serving my country. I went back to college and received my master's degree in business and minored in US history.

I would like a fair opportunity to use my degree and real-world experience in supply chain management in your company. I am intrigued by your company's excellent reputation as an innovator in material distribution.

With both military and civilian experience, I am qualified to operate military material management software. I can learn and be trained quickly.

I have trained over one hundred (100) employees in different job opportunities. I am well-traveled my results will be nothing but positive while working under pressure with strong concentrations.

I can exercise sound judgment from start to completion of my work. At the end of the day saving my company monies just like I did before I decided to cross over to the civilian workforce.

I believe my education; work ethics, and ability to adapt and overcome would allow me to contribute productively in achieving your company's immediate goals.

Sir or Madam, I hope I may call your office to see if you could schedule some time to see me and discuss my qualifications to help improve your organizations goals.

My résumé is attached to this cover letter for your review. In advance, I am grateful for your time and look forward to hearing from you.

Sincerely, *Eric Brown*

## A Cover Letter True Story:

IT WAS SIX O'CLOCK: AND I had just about given up for that day with job searching. It was a hot day, my car didn't' air-conditioning, the heat made my white starched shirt wrinkled badly from getting in and out of the hot car.

I walked up to lady, spoke with her for a short moment, and gave her my phone number and cover letter and résumé. I got lucky that day I got me an interview and a job offer with her company with my one page smart résumé, One week later my new employer asked me to relocate to Michigan project. I said "but really I did not want to travel that far away from home for a job.

The previous day at six o'clock on Friday, I placed my one page résumé and cover letter between the doors at a company named Zeus. The doors were locked, and I realized all the personnel had gone for the weekend.

I had only one week to find a job to stay home or I was leaving for Michigan. I waited for Zeus's Human Resources to call me for an interview. I continued to work and planned to relocate to Michigan. Two weeks later, there had been no response from Zeus, and now it was Friday, my last day in town.

After two weeks on my new job, I got the call I was waiting for; it was Zeus's Human Resources. The voice said to me, "Mr. Weston, "we found your résumé, and I want to interview you". "Can you come in for an interview tomorrow?"

I said, "No, sir." I would love to, but I am living in Michigan now." I asked him if he could be so kind as to interview me over the cell- phone."

He said, "We can't interview you over the phone, Mr. Weston."

I asked him to put my interview on hold until I returned to South Carolina the next year, and he said "I will try."

After that phone call ended, I began to think about leaving the Michigan project. I was working at my desk; it was 6:00 p.m. and I had the blues. But I decided to stay and work in Michigan. I began to unpack my things for a one year stay.

One more story about a résumé and cover letter; a lady who lived in South Carolina said on the local news she was fed up with driving around looking for job interviews. So she attached her one-page résumés and cover letter to balloons turned the balloons into the winds, and let them fly away. I do not know if she ever got contacted for a job interview, but she put a creative thought to work in hopes of gaining employment.

## CHAPTER 22

# Key Management Leadership and Organizational Skills List

| | | |
|---|---|---|
| Administered | Executed | Produced |
| Approved | Handled | Provided |
| Arranged | Headed | Recommended |
| Classified | Inspected | Recorded |
| Compiled | Led | Reviewed |
| Conceptualized | Maintained | Scheduled |
| Converted | Managed | Selected |
| Corrected | Monitored | Streamlined |
| Delegated | Motivated | Supervised |
| Developed | Operated | Supplied |
| Directed | Organized | Terminated |
| Enforced | Oversaw | Updated |
| Enhanced | Planned | Validated |
| Established | Prioritized | |

CHAPTER 23

# My Final Thoughts
# on Leadership:

As a supervisor, you do not always get to select your own team players.
Sometimes you have to play the hand that is dealt to you.

Put yourself in the authority's shoes. Today you must interview
and hire someone for a full-time position. Which person will you hire?
They all have the same college degree, they are equally diverse, and each
seems to be trainable. Would you hire the former Job Corps person, the
former military person, or the recent college graduate? It's not an easy
choice to make.

One thing for sure is that if you are perceived to be a trainable, likable
person during your interview, the company will hire you regardless of
job market conditions.

If leaders are not keeping employees happy and trained, it is because
they do not know any better, or they do not care about training until
something goes wrong. That is an example of bad management.

Employees choose to be engaging, especially if you're the type of leader who tends to help the employees with more than just their jobs. Quality control covers people, as well as products, services, and processes. It ensures a certain level of quality through leader inputs and outputs. The old way of doing things will eventually fade away. The workforces will call for a different, more caring leader who must be relatable to human needs on and outside the job.

Supervisors will never be able to predict what kinds of conflicts they will encounter. They must be able to deal with employees and ensure the stress does not carry over in their relations with others. Leaders who have low levels of stress have happier employees.

*Do Nothing-Leaders:* This type of leader, figuratively speaking, will sit and wait and see what develop; he or she will want to implement fast solutions to workplace problems, having waited until it's almost too late, unless it's going to benefit him or her. Do-nothing leaders are weak leaders: they will have problems empowering their employees. They try to avoid being in tough decision making situations. They are afraid to address workplace problems right away, and they will select employees they can control to get information for them.

*Team Leaders:* Team leaders are an important link to the management team and workforce process. The team leader steps in day today and gives professional guidance and takes over for supervisors when they are not around. Team leaders are sometimes the best candidates to select for supervisor position. They share responsibility with supervisors and managers in monitoring and developing employees; by spot checking employees' work progress through the use of their quality system. Team leaders can have a positive impact on award recommendations, performance evaluation reports, and disciplinary actions.

*Mentors:* Mentors are more experienced than we are, and this is why we seek their wisdom. The mentor will take your learning curve to a much higher level of understanding, further than if a person tried to figure out things for himself or herself. A mentor is a coach, and he or she teaches knowledge to grow on that makes a positive impact in your life, but be carefully in selecting whom you will share your career problems and concerns with in order to select your own mentor.

*Parents:* Parents are leaders also; they can be more like a live-in mentors. They are our biggest supporters. Our parents give us the stability, security, basic training, and love we need to become successful productive citizens. They are our insurance policies when we cannot make it on our own. Leadership starts at home. What we learn in our home determines how we bond and how we treat people outside our home.

*Wisdom to Live By:* A young army officer who supervised me wrote the following statement "It is essential that people be able to work together, moreover, it is equally important to an employee to feel appreciated in his or her workplace". So leader's responsibility to their employees is to take care of them." That officer would become my commander.

*Proverbs 29:18 (King James Version, (KJV):* "Where there is no vision, the people perish but he that keeps the law, happy is he."

CPSIA information can be obtained at www.ICGtesting.com
Printed in the USA
BVOW04*0251030916

460670BV00013B/3/P